MAN
WITH
CAMERA

MAN WITH CAMERA

PHOTOGRAPHS FROM SEVEN DECADES

BY

FELIX H. MAN

SCHOCKEN BOOKS

NEW YORK

First American edition published by Schocken Books 1984

10 9 8 7 6 5 4 3 2 1   84 85 86 87

Published by agreement with Martin Secker & Warburg, London

Library of Congress Cataloging in Publication Data
Man, Felix H., 1893–
  Man with camera.
  1. Photography—Portraits.   2. Man, Felix H.,
  1893–   . I. Title.
  TR681.F3M37   1984   770'.92'4   83–7387

Printed in Great Britain by
BAS Printers Limited, Over Wallop, Hampshire

ISBN 0–8052–3877–8

Introduction

Kokoschka was right when he called the Salzburg Academy 'School of Vision'. It is the art of seeing that is important—and this is something which changes with time.

The pioneers of what came to be known as photo-journalism developed a new way of seeing in photography. This not only resulted in the essay, using a camera instead of a pen to describe a situation, but led on to a new conception, in which photographers abandoned the static picture. They made their main task the capture of the fleeting instant, called by Lessing, in his *Laokoon*, 'the fruitful moment' in which the natural surroundings were carefully preserved. To present the essence of a happening, without altering or disturbing the natural atmospheric conditions, these photographers used methods that were entirely new. Thus they developed a new style, and opened new fields for indoor photography, still unknown in those days, and today fully exploited by the television camera. They became the initiators of a new way of seeing, by creating a form of photography which has lasted to the present day—though often watered down.

It has often been said that the camera, as a mechanical instrument, can only record what is there. This is true. But not everybody can see what is there, and creative minds will use 'the little glass eye' with quite different results, which cannot be compared with the optical appearance. Naturally the 'candid camera' had to make use of outward appearances; but also the great difference in this new interpretation was not only that it was selective to the highest degree, but that, if the task was to photograph human beings, this task was approached in an entirely new way, returning to simplicity, rejecting all artificial means, and emphasising psychological factors.

In general, portrait photography has developed from rather primitive but honest beginnings into an industry practised mostly in the uncomfortable atmosphere of the studio, where the wretched sitter is surrounded by powerful lights designed to bring out his features in the most flattering form. This technique produces no more than counterfeit portraits, with light and shade 'artistically' pronounced, resulting in a lifeless replica of the sitter, who has been forced into a certain position which, while perhaps well observed, reveals itself in the end as a theatrical pose, lacking any real life and spirit.

With the new interpretation, the sitter was made to feel at ease and comfortable in his own surroundings. He was given no directions, his normal activities were not disturbed, and the normal atmosphere of his way of life was preserved. At the same time, personal contact had to be established, and photographs taken at unobserved and crucial moments, reached through long and close observation and the utmost concentration.

It was not easy to fulfil all these tasks more than fifty years ago, when many technical problems had to be surmounted. In spite of the 'Ermanox' camera, with a lens with an aperture of 1:1.8, if indoor photographs were had to be taken by available light, or if people in action such as conductors were to be photographed, it has to be remembered that negative sensitivities then were only a fraction of what they are today. The present-day photographer knows nothing of these difficulties, as all these problems have been solved mechanically— usually to the disadvantage of the eventual result. In the early days, with the limited means at our disposal, it was nearly always the rule that the negative was under-exposed, and had to be reinforced after development, in spite of the fact that exposure times varied between one-half and one-eighth of a second. For this reason, all indoor photographs had to be taken with a tripod, as it was impossible to hold the camera steady. No light or distance meters were available. Distances had to be estimated, and only on rare occasions was it possible to look through the viewfinder, and never possible to control the picture on the matt-screen.

The number of photographs we could take was limited, as we had to work with glass plates in metal cassettes; as a rule, not more than 15 to 20 of these could be carried on an assignment. We hardly ever exposed more than one negative of the same subject. We did not then conform to Bernard Shaw's idea that 'the photographer is like a cod-fish who lays a million eggs in the hope that one may hatch'—an idea which makes more sense today, when photographers may take 300–500 pictures for one story, of which perhaps 20 or so will be selected later by the editor who has encouraged these methods. The technical limitations of the early days demanded great concentration and creative capacity. Each exposure had to be a hit.

In those early days, the photographer was not regarded as a nuisance; he was invited as a guest, and worked alone, dressed, on festive occasions, in tails like the other guests.

A clear distinction should be made between documentary photography and pictorial journalism. Documentary photography as practised, for instance, by Jacob Riis or Lewis Hine, was something different, as these forerunners did not comply with some of the principles observed by the pictorial journalists. For technical reasons, their photographs had to be posed, or taken by flashlight, both spoiling the real atmosphere. Masters such as Stieglitz, Paul Martin or Sir Benjamin Stone, who brought a new note into picture-taking, certainly took photographs in unguarded moments, but their range was limited to outdoor photography, and did not include the photo-essay. (Nadar's photo-interview with Chevreuil is an exception.)

Photo-journalism was in its prime in the years 1929 to 1932 when, unburdened by modern technical gadgets, a few protagonists—none of them professional photographers—achieved epoch-making results. These had their origin in creativity, and were true to the thought that the quality or the artistic merit of a photograph is not dependent on the subject, nor on the technique used, nor on any preconceived idea, but only on its radiative power.

In those early days, a photo-essay was usually given only two pages in a weekly magazine. Strict condensation of the theme was necessary. In later years, magazines gave five or more pages to an essay, not always to the advantage of the theme.

How I came to photography

Modern medical science has clearly established that impressions we get in our early youth not only follow us through life, but have a decisive influence on our future development. I recall vividly the first encounter I had with a professional photographer.

This happened about the turn of the century in the small provincial town of Freiburg i.B. in Southern Germany where I was born. Life in this place was dominated by retired colonels, former university professors, industrialists and other well-to-do people who had chosen this spot for their retirement, in the mild climate and beautiful vine-growing country at the foot of the Black Forest. On the other hand, the two thousand or more university students there offered a guarantee that the 'life without haste' of the ordinary citizen never became completely stagnant. The town was very romantic and picturesque, with many Gothic and Renaissance buildings. Through almost every street in the old quarter ran small rivulets, a peculiarity carefully preserved by the town authorities.

In those days, traffic was insignificant in such a town. Electric trams did not yet exist, and the buses were horse-drawn. Although the home town of Karl Benz, inventor of the motor car, was only two hundred miles away, there were less than half-a-dozen cars in the town, and they were then known as *Benzinwagen*. These only appeared on special occasions in mid-summer, when they attempted, not always successfully, to drive up the *Höllental* into the Black Forest, where they were looked upon by the peasants as engines of the devil.

It is understandable that, when our teacher told us that a photographer was to take a picture of the class the next day, we all got very excited at the prospect; at that time we were not yet spoiled by the cinema and other optical illusions.

We explained to our parents the importance of the occasion, for which we had been told to put on our Sunday suits. I was up earlier than usual the next morning, as I could not sleep for excitement. I dressed very carefully in my best clothes, under my mother's watchful eye.

We assembled in the corridor outside our class room, where our master was waiting for us, keeping the livelier boys in order. We eagerly listened to what was going on behind the closed doors, screening the secrets which were dominating our minds.

Finally we were called in. We were about 30 boys, all aged six or seven, and we rushed in the moment the doors were opened. But the two men there, and our teacher, did not give us a chance to explore the setting which the photographer had built up. We were assembled on the large rostrum in front of the blackboard, where the length of the wall had been covered with a white cloth. In half-an-hour's hard work, the photographer, with the teacher's help, arranged a fantastic group, taking care that every boy was clearly visible. I was placed near the front, on the left of the group, and given a ball, which I was to pretend to throw to another boy, on the opposite side, who was to pretend to catch it. But, when I turned to the right, so that I could see my 'target', I was rebuked by the photographer, and made to turn to face the camera, like everybody else, with my right arm stretched out with the ball. Although this seemed stupid to me, I did not dare move again, until I got tired and dropped the ball.

During the lengthy preparations, I had been watching the photographer carefully, seeing how he disappeared repeatedly under his large black cloth behind his enormous three-legged box, while his assistant, standing on a ladder, fumbled with something undefined on the top of a long brass rod, which nearly touched the ceiling and looked like a pan. Then I noticed him emptying a bottle of greyish-white powder into this pan, and climbing down the ladder. At this point our teacher clapped his hands for silence, and the photographer who, I have forgotten to mention, held the title of 'Court-Photographer', made a speech. He told us that there was nothing to be frightened of, and that when there was a sudden flash of very bright light, like lightning, we should all look straight into the camera, and not close our eyes. The flash was meant to occur when he had counted up to three. But, although we were all standing motionless, with our eyes open, nothing happened when he reached three. The assistant pulled the string attached to the top of the brass rod again and again—I had counted on up to twenty, when everything was called off for the time being. Up the ladder went the assistant—a lot of fiddling about followed—again our teacher clapped for silence—the group was rearranged as before—all looked at the camera—one-two-three—a big flash—and the room was filled with a biting smoke, and we had to open the windows to stop us from coughing. The picture was inside the magic box.

Today there is nothing strange in meeting an eleven-year-old boy with a camera, but, when I was about that age, I was very excited to meet my best friend's cousin, who had come from the 'far North'—Hamburg—to spend his summer holiday in our small southern town. He owned a box camera, and knew how to use it, although he was only a little older than myself. I pleaded with my father until I too was the owner of a Box-Kodak, a simple contraption, then costing only ten marks—about the equivalent of ten shillings.

For the rest of the school holidays I had no time for anything else. I photographed everything—houses, trees, dogs, cats, all my friends, in fact anything that would keep still. It was not long before I had mastered all the secrets of my little toy box, and soon I was even able to take landscapes with cloud effects.

However I very soon realised that my modest pocket-money was not going to be enough to buy the films, and pay for developing and printing, in spite of my foregoing all other pleasures. My father had to step in again. He was very interested in chemistry, and had taken his Doctor's degree in this science, as a hobby, at the age of forty. He bought me some small dishes, bottles and measures, and the cheapest dark-room lamp on the market, so that I could set up a dark-room laboratory in the cellar of our house. As we had no electricity, gas being then the usual form of lighting, and as paraffin was, in my father's opinion, explosive and highly dangerous, my dark-room lamp—oiled red canvas over a metal frame—was lit by a candle. It was no doubt primitive, but it worked.

There was a place in our cellar, under the stairs, which I knew well from games of hide-and-seek. Though without a door, this corner was completely dark, as one had to turn three corners to reach it. Here I watched for the first time the miracle of a picture appearing on the creamy surface of the film under my own hands.

As time went on, I learnt the different methods of printing a negative: in the sun, in the shade, and by gaslight. It was the fashion at this time to tone the prints brown, green or blue. But, after about three years, I felt a great dissatisfaction with the obvious limitations of the box-camera. I discarded photography completely, and started to draw, to paint and to etch. I was strongly encouraged by the school drawing-master, an artist who had exhibited at the *Kunstverein*, of which my father was an enthusiastic member, and where I had seen, for the first time, paintings by Renoir, Cézanne and Toulouse-Lautrec.

Our town, though very provincial and with only 75,000 inhabitants, was a real centre of culture. The permanent Opera House, to which the world's greatest singers came as guest-artists, was regarded as a sort of springboard to the *Hof-Theaters* of Berlin, Dresden or Munich, and had an annual subsidy from the town of several hundred thousand marks, to maintain its high standards. My father was a great music-lover; he had known Richard Wagner, and had visited Bayreuth from its inception. He had for many years been the music critic of the *Rigaer Tageblatt*, the leading newspaper of his Baltic home town, then under Russian Tsarist rule. This was, of course, a side-line, as he was in fact a banker, having inherited the family business in Riga from my grandfather. Consequently, we had our own box at the *Stadttheater*, and I got acquainted at a very early age with the Italian and German masterpieces, from Mozart to Richard Strauss. The musical life of the town was of a very high standard; concerts given by the very best people took place almost every week. Even Caruso nearly came there, but decided at the last moment to give his concert at Baden-Baden, the spa fifty miles away—but a special train was arranged, so we did not miss this event.

One incident in our musical life has remained vividly in my memory. I must have been about five years old when Johann Strauss's son conducted at a big open-air concert in the Stadtgarten on a wonderful summer's evening. The gardens were still lit by gaslight in an unobtrusive and comfortable way, creating a romantic atmosphere. I remember this special event as my parents persuaded me to accept a bottle of fizzy lemonade as consolation for staying at home while the rest of the family went to hear the *Walzerking* conduct extracts from *Die Fledermaus* and *Geschichten aus dem Wiener Wald*.

Painting and drawing kept me completely occupied, and gave me such pleasure that I no longer considered the camera as a suitable means of expressing myself. Only once did I take my old box-camera out, and then I nearly took my first news picture—and it was through no fault of mine that it did not materialise in the end.

Germany was Zeppelin-crazy at this time. When it became known that the Graf with his airship was to make his first long-distance trip from Lake Constance, down the Rhine to Frankfurt, half our town made the fifteen-mile pilgrimage, in the early morning, to witness this memorable triumph from the banks of the Rhine. There we picnicked and waited all day, looking expectantly southwards towards Basle, where the Rhine turns from west to north. But at nightfall we all had to return disappointed, when we learnt that the 'Big Cigar' could not make it that day, and it was not certain when it would come. The airship in fact turned up a few days later, and flew around our town, but in those pre-wireless days, this was a complete surprise, and I did not have my box-camera with me.

I decided fairly early to become a painter, but my father insisted that I should stay at school until the end, and pass my matriculation exams. The last two years at school seemed rather hard to me and to some of my friends, and we enlivened the boredom by gate-crashing the university, where we attended late afternoon and evening lectures on philosophy, literature, fine-arts and psychology. This was naturally against all the rules, but the professors accepted the *schinden*, as it was called, as they preferred a 'full house'. The end of my school days meant leaving home to study painting, first in Munich, and then in Berlin. But these studies were brusquely interrupted in the summer of 1914 by World War I. I joined the army and, after some fighting in Northern France, I was moved to Alsace, to the Upper Rhine valley, where the trenches were only about 30 miles from home. It was then that I remembered my old box-camera, but a search proved fruitless and I bought a 'Vest-Pocket Kodak' which, from then on, I used in the front-line trenches on quiet days. Using this small hand-camera, I acquired thorough technical knowledge and practical experience, never using an exposure meter or a calculator. All my original negatives from this time were unfortunately lost, and only a few contact prints survived, from which copy-negatives have been made.

In this sector of the front, the war was not too hard on me. My Quartermaster-Sergeant also came from my home town—I was by now an officer—and we used to go home in turn at weekends, bicycling without lights to avoid the attentions of the military police.

The end of the war meant the end of photographic activity. I moved back to Munich to complete my studies.

1915 All quiet on the Alsatian front. At this time, the old *Pickelhaube* helmet was still being worn as protection; steel helmets were not yet in use.

1915 On look-out. Although there was a lull in the fighting, no-man's-land between the two front lines was constantly watched; snipers fired occasional shots.

1915 Commanding Officer's dug-out. With the villages behind the line destroyed, and their inhabitants gone, the possessions which had survived the shelling were used to furnish the dug-outs in the front line.

1915 Devastated village in Alsace. By the spring of 1915, the front lines had been established in southern Alsace, and the trenches dug. There was a lull in the fighting lasting many weeks, when only occasional single shots were fired. The soldiers in the trenches either enjoyed the spring weather, or made improvements to their dug-outs.

Berlin at the end of the Twenties

Towards the end of the twenties, Berlin, then the capital of the Weimar Republic, was *the* town of Germany. In the days of the Emperor William II, the court had dominated life in Berlin too much to allow liberal and free development, and to make Berlin the centre of German cultural and artistic life. But about ten years after the end of World War I, things had changed completely, and the cultural events of the German capital were unsurpassed.

There were three opera houses of the very first class, with conductors like Kleiber, Bruno Walter, Klemperer and Furtwängler, with his Philharmonic Orchestra. In the *Deutsches Theater*, Max Reinhardt was the reigning figure, and a first night with Werner Krauss or Elisabeth Bergner was not only an artistic event of great importance, but a society event with tails and gala evening dresses, and the presence of leading figures from the diplomatic world, from the arts and from politics, writers such as Heinrich Mann, Gottfried Benn and Alfred Döblin, and scientists like Einstein and Max Planck. Next morning the sharp and much-feared critic Alfred Kerr gave his résumé in the *Berliner Tageblatt*, in his own peculiar style, with paragraphs headed by Roman numerals. In those days Kerr was as important a critic in Berlin as James Agate was in London, or Hazlitt had been in Regency days.

Then there was the *Volksbühne* with Erwin Piscator and his progressive, proletarian theatre, orientated towards the East, and much praised by the salon-communists. Many thousands of these lived in Berlin, for it was almost *de rigueur* to acknowledge Karl Marx as a patron saint, as a kind of counterbalance to the growing Hitlerism; the Weill-Brecht version of *The Beggar's Opera* was not sold out every evening solely on account of its artistic merit.

Those who preferred less serious music could applaud Franz Lehár or Oskar Strauss conducting their operettas at the *Metropole Theater*, and listen to the melting tenor voice of Richard Tauber, singing love-songs.

Around the *Gedächtniskirche* in the West End, and on *Kurfürstendamm* were the haunts of the avant-garde, and nightlife flourished. Discussion went on until the early hours at the *Romanische Café*, the meeting-place of intellectuals and bohemians, while on an upper floor the world chess-master Emanuel Lasker gave demonstrations of this royal game. Customarily one looked in at the *Romanische* at least once during an evening, if only to eat a couple of eggs in a glass before going home at about three in the morning, to restore the balance of soul and body after a full night.

The gastronomic pleasures of the capital were not be despised, as there was a choice of first-class restaurants. But those without much money could go at any time to one of the *Aschinger Bierquelle* restaurant chain, to fill himself with *Löffelerbsen mit Speck* for 25 *Pfennig*, on top of which he could eat as many rolls as he wished free of charge.

Before World War II, Berlin was a metropolis in the midst of greenery, surrounded by pine woods and lakes. It was a town of charm and soul, with pace but without haste. The horse-drawn bus no longer plied from Potsdammer Platz to the Friedrichstrasse Station for five *Pfennig*, but the street girls in their red and green knee-length boots still waited nightly at the corner of the Jägerstrasse.

On mild summer evenings, one went to *Spree-Garten* for a special beer—*Berliner Weisse*—and listened to Paul Linke's *Glow Worm*, a favourite melody of the day; or one went to see the popular musical clown Caro at the open-air theatre. In half-an-hour one could reach the Havel, or the Grunewald, or one could swim, or sail on the Wannsee. In winter one could skate for miles on the lakes.

In short, Berlin was *the* town of Germany. And as it was not only the capital of the Republic, but the trade and banking centre, with the head-quarters of the big industries, and as it was a cultural and intellectual centre rivalling Munich, everybody with ambition sooner or later directed his steps towards Berlin. I did this in 1926.

Many think themselves appointed, but only a few are selected. My career as a painter was of no importance, and it was a good thing that I had sufficient self-criticism to realise this fact for myself, and therefore developed the more practical side of my profession. I had started to illustrate, and became a regular contributor to the Berlin daily paper *B–Z am Mittag*, published by the House of Ullstein; the paper also had a Sunday edition and carried many illustrations.

As the paper was published at noon, the deadline for the illustrations was eight in the morning. This meant working at night, finishing my illustrations, working from sketches done in the afternoon. The illustrations had to be accurate, and I had the idea of using my camera, in retirement since the war, to refresh my memory.

After a few months, I noticed that technical progress meant that newspapers were starting to use more photographs, and it became more economical for me to let them have my photographs, instead of using them as a basis for an illustration. I was gradually sliding into a new profession, supplying photographs, not only to *B–Z am Mittag*, but dailies like *Tempo* and *Morgenpost*. My photographs were fresh in style and conception, and they were eagerly accepted by other journals, and attracted the attention of the Editor of a newly-founded agency, *Deutscher Photo-Dienst* or *DEPHOT*. This was Simon Gutmann; through him I met Stefan Lorant, then Berlin Editor of the *Münchner Illustrierte Presse*. He at once asked me to photograph two essays for his magazine, a task at which three photographers he had commissioned had failed. I was able to do both essays to his satisfaction, and so got a contract with this illustrated journal. My contract stipulated that, although I got a monthly guarantee, I was to be paid 300 marks for every page contributed, in addition to travelling expenses. This was a fabulous amount, and an extraordinary position. In the next three years I contributed nearly 250 pages as their principal photo-journalist. I was allowed to accept commissions from the *Berliner Illustrierte*, for whom I also travelled.

When these connections began in 1929, I was practically without any competition. My camera was, nearly always, the only one at an important private or public function. My little glass eye was at home everywhere, in the palaces of Heads of State, or in the miserable homes of penniless hand-weavers. Though my main contract was with a Munich paper, I kept my headquarters in Berlin, and travelled from there as needed. Berlin itself offered many aspects of daily life not previously photographed—Kurfürstendamm after midnight, a concert with Casals at Charlottenburg Castle by candlelight, trotting-races by night, an important art auction—all these were among the themes unexplored by the camera, and made possible only by my new methods and the tripod.

However my chief interest was the human being, the great personalities of the epoch; I travelled by sleeper all over Europe, constantly on the look-out for new impressions, typical of the country, but totally unknown to the average reader. What was a novelty from an unexplored region fifty years ago, has today become a general possession, in particular since television began to show millions of people things which in earlier days could only be experienced by a privileged few.

1929 Max Reinhardt First Night. A Max Reinhardt First Night at the *Deutsches Theater* in Berlin was always the event of the season. The *Prominenz* who attended in white tie and tails not only wanted to see a play by Bernard Shaw, but also wanted to be seen. The President of the Reichstag, the French, British and American Ambassadors, and great financiers were in the boxes and the Grand Tier. In those days, the audience were still dimly lit by old-fashioned lamps; spotlights were not yet in use. Naturally it was difficult to photograph the audience in this diffused light, and a tripod had to be used.

1931 Kroll Opera First Night. Hans Pfitzner's *Das Herz* was first performed at the Kroll Opera in 1931, Bruno Walter conducting. Pfitzner, best known for his opera *Palestrina*, was not a very popular composer, even in Germany; when his music was first heard in London, the music critic of the *Times* wrote: 'For the first and, we hope, the last time, we have heard the music of the German composer Pfitzner. . .' Bruno Walter was best known as a conductor of Mozart, and was for many years musical director of the Munich State Opera; he left Germany when Hitler came to power.

1929 Evening Reception in the Film world. Towards the end of the twenties, evening receptions for the press and the film world were one of the features of society life, attended only in formal clothes. These were exclusive occasions, attended by such important stars as Willy Fritsch, Hans Albers, Lilian Harvey, Brigitte Helm and Leni Riefenstahl, who became prominent during the Hitler regime. Well-known directors such as G. W. Pabst and Fritz Lang would attend, with well-known people from art and politics.

1929 Kurfürstendamm after midnight. In the days of Wilhelm II, *Under den Linden* was the haunt of society. During the Weimar Republic, *Kurfürstendamm* took its place as the pulse-centre of the capital. Here were the night clubs, the cabarets, and the fashionable restaurants and cafés. The night life continued till early dawn, when the man with a long stick came round switching off the street gas-lights.

1930 Candlelit Concert at Charlottenburg. As early as 1930 Pablo Casals was a cellist with a world-wide reputation. With Frederick Lamond as accompanist, he gave a concert at Charlottenburg Castle, which had neither gas nor electric light. The wax candles in the chandelier gave a diffused light, so a tripod was required for this photograph.

1929 Jazz Band in a palais, Berlin. The jazz band as a dance team, instead of a violinist and a piano, was still a novelty in 1929, but soon this new type of entertainment was accepted at evening parties in elegant homes.

1936 Casals as soloist, London. Alongside Pablo Casals at a Queen's Hall concert, with Sir Adrian Boult conducting. The very progressive Sir Adrian allowed me, for the first time in London, to sit with my camera and tripod in the middle of the orchestra; the audience probably thought I was playing a new instrument.

1930 Toscanini at Bayreuth. The 1930 season at Bayreuth was dominated by Arturo Toscanini. Siegfried Wagner, the composer's son, was still directing the opera house; he died the same year. Lauritz Melchior, Rudolf Bockelmann and Hanny Larsen-Todsen listen to the *maestro* at the piano, singing a passage which one of the singers had not performed to his satisfaction.

1930 Toscanini rehearsing. At this time,
Toscanini hated the press and refused to be
photographed. This early picture of the *maestro*
in the orchestra pit was taken secretly from the
stage, through a hole in the curtain.

1930 Siegfried Wagner, son of Richard, directing.

1930 Swimming rehearsal for Rhinemaidens, Bayreuth.

1930 Double-bass after rehearsal, Berlin Philharmonic Orchestra.

1931 Paul von Hindenburg, President of the Weimar Republic, in his study, Berlin.

1930/31 Papal Nuncio Orsenigo addresses Hindenburg at the New Year reception for the Diplomatic Corps.

1930 Professor Max Planck in his Berlin Home. The Nobel-prize winner Max Planck, physicist and originator of the 'Quantum Theory' which altered the concepts of physics, was old-fashioned in appearance and preferred to work at a standing-desk. Next to Einstein, Planck was one of the most important scientists of his time.

1930 Max Liebermann painting a self-portrait. Liebermann, a leading German Impressionist, also known as a portrait painter, had studied in Paris. He painted and etched several self-portraits. The photograph ('Three times Liebermann') shows the eighty-three year old at work in his Berlin studio.

1930 Liebermann in a typical hard-of-hearing gesture.

1931 Max Slevogt at the window of his house. Slevogt, an important artist in Germany at this time, was an Impressionist with a romantic tendency, and was also known as a portrait painter.

1931 Slevogt in his studio, Berlin.

1930 The Munich comedian Weiss-Ferdl. Weiss-Ferdl, a popular comedian, in his dressing-room, preparing for the stage.

1930 The Berlin comedian 'Caro'. 'Caro' appeared on an open-air stage in the *Spree-Garten* with his public sitting at tables drinking beer.

1930 A corner of Weiss-Ferdl's dressing room.

1930 Blast-furnace at the Haniel Steel Works, Rhineland. Fireworks of a kind as boiling liquid steel is moved by big cranes and made to flow into forms. The occupation of the 'Ruhr' by French troops from 1923 to 1930, to prevent the rearming of Germany, was one of the reasons why the numbers of unemployed in Germany had risen to 6 million by the end of 1932; and unemployment was in turn one of the reasons why the Nazis won 40% of the seats in the Reichstag in that year.

1930 Steel furnace at Siemenstadt, Berlin. Before World War II, Siemenstadt was one of the largest industrial complexes in Germany, and the headquarters of the Siemens electrical concern.

1930 Foundry at Siemenstadt.

1930 The home of a workless hand-weaver in Upper Silesia during the Depression.

1930 A workless hand-weaver in the Glatzer mountains. Hand-weavers were hit especially hard by the Depression of 1930, since their work had suffered already with the introduction of the mechanical loom. Their fate had already been described in a play by Gerhard Hauptmann, and Käthe Kollwitz immortalised them in her graphic work.

1930 Workroom and nursery are the same for the Glatzer mountain hand-weaver.

1930 Preparing the warp.

1930 The meagre fare of the hand-weaver's family—bread, potato and water.

1929 Metzgerbräu Beercellar, Munich. Brass bands and weightlifting were features of the Munich beercellars of this time; *Metzgerbräu* was one of the best known. *Gemütlichkeit* reigned supreme. Strong men met to lift weights up to 100 kilos, while the visitors enjoyed their beer. It was in beercellars of this kind that Hitler had had his meetings in the twenties, being nearly assassinated on one occasion.

1929 Weightlifting, Metzgerbräu. Having managed to lift the weight, the strong man drops it a moment later.

1929 Nürburgring. Changing the wheel of the racing ace Lepori's Bugatti. This was the inaugural race-meeting at the circuit.

1929 Trotting Race at Berlin-Mariendorf. Trotting racing, by night and with artificial light, was a favourite Berlin pastime. (Montage)

1929 Lunapark, Berlin. Lunapark was not only an amusement centre; you could refresh yourself in a large indoor swimming pool with artificial waves. The pool was open until midnight, and in the surrounding boxes people in evening dress were dining.

1929 Lunapark. Beside the swimming pool there were terraces for sunbathing.

1931 Charlie Chaplin visiting the Berlin slums. Dr Edgar Stern-Rubarth is standing next to Chaplin.

1930 Cloakroom Attendant, Harnack House, Berlin.

1929 Term starts at Berlin University. Students hold a *Steh Konvent* in the forecourt.

1929 Term starts at Berlin University. Studying announcements on the students' noticeboard.

1930 Berlin at three in the morning. The guests have left the Romanische Café, a haunt of intellectuals, and the waiters clear the table.

Meeting the famous

People in an envious mood have often said to me 'What a wonderful life you must have, travelling the world in luxury, meeting the famous.' Indeed, to look back on the life of a photo-journalist, attached to one of the big illustrated papers, is to look back on a life of many adventures and priceless experiences. Sometimes the editor just said the magic words 'Go and bring back what you find'—which in practice meant travelling to the unknown, perhaps exploring unmapped territory. Though I have always been interested in human beings, and especially the great personalities of our time, some of these journeys into the unknown remain the most treasured memories of my professional life. However, photographing the great personalities of the day is one of the most rewarding tasks for the creative photographer.

In the late Twenties and early Thirties, statesmen of all nations tried to bring some order into Europe's tangled affairs by holding international conferences, at The Hague, at Geneva, at Locarno and elsewhere. Men like Stresemann and Briand were full of hope that the two old enemies, France and Germany, had buried the hatchet for ever. In 1931 the French Prime Minister, Laval, with his Foreign Minister Briand, paid a State visit to Berlin, the first such visit since the war of 1870. Stresemann had died, but Chancellor Brüning continued to pursue a policy of understanding with France. I went to Paris, in order to be able to travel back to Berlin with the French Ministers in their special train; I had been received by Briand a few hours earlier in the privacy of his study at the Quai d'Orsay.

By this time, I had become accustomed to such privileges. As early as 1930, I had been asked by the German President von Hindenburg, to photograph him in his study, in his Palais in the Wilhelmstrasse in Berlin. I owed this favour to the fact that the aged President disliked both lamps and flashlights, and he had heard that I used neither. He allowed me a quarter-of-an-hour in the early morning; as I had first to get him at ease, most of this time was spent in talk, he asking me whether I had been a soldier, and questioning me about the war. It was difficult to photograph the Field Marshal without posing him, so I pretended to take some photographs, and then suggested that he should continue with his work, as there were many papers on his desk. Thinking that I had finished, he turned to his papers, and I was able at once to take the picture I wanted.

I had another session with Hindenburg about two years later, in 1931, a few months before he was re-elected for a second term as President of Germany. Secretary of State Meissner, then the power in the Palais, had not told the old gentleman anything about my coming, but the photographs were badly needed for the election campaign. Hindenburg was somewhat annoyed by my surprise visit, a fact he only partly concealed—'Well—I know—it is not your fault that you are here again—it is only your duty to do your job—and so—I shall do my duty—let us go ahead.' A photograph of him, standing upright, was displayed in 1932, about four times life-size, on the roofs of the Potsdammer Platz, and helped him to win the election against Hitler.

From time to time I accepted commisions from the *Berliner Illustrierte*, as my agreement with Munich did not preclude this. I went, for them, to Bayreuth in 1930, where Toscanini was rehearsing for the Festival with some of the world's most famous singers. Cosima Wagner, the guardian of Bayreuth, had died the previous year; Richard Wagner's son Siegfried, and his wife Winifred, were directing the *Festspielhaus*. My request to photograph Toscanini rehearsing was turned down by the Wagners, who knew the *maestro's* temperamental outbursts only too well. Toscanini had an aversion to journalists and to photographers in particular; this went so far that he used to cover his face with his hat, like Greta Garbo, when he saw a photographer in the street. Although world-famous, Toscanini had not at this time been through the American publicity mill.

When I suggested photographing him rehearsing in the orchestra pit, assuring him that he would not be disturbed in any way, he flatly refused; knowing his temperament, I did not dare to hide amongst the players in the pit. But luck was with me, when I learnt that he was to have a piano rehearsal the next day, in a private house, with some of the soloists. I was wondering how I could make use of this information, when Wotan came to my rescue—Wotan being the famous bass Rudolf Bockelmann, who became greatly interested in my project.

The music-room at the villa where the rehearsal was to take place was connected with an adjoining room by a large sliding door. Following our plan, Bockelmann went last into the music-room, leaving a small gap in the sliding doors, just big enough for me to look through without being noticed. I fixed my Ermanox camera on its tripod, and quickly took some pictures of the scene. I was about to pack up and slip away, when I heard Toscanini's voice raised in anger. At first I thought I was the cause of his annoyance, but soon understood that he was criticising some of the singers. Suddenly, to make himself clear, he started to sing himself, while playing the piano. I quickly readjusted the camera, and a unique photograph of Toscanini singing at the piano was the result.

Encouraged by this success, I risked hiding on the stage the next day, and through a small hole photographed the *maestro* rehearsing in the orchestra pit, probably the first photograph of the famous musician conducting.

In pre-Hitler days, the leading German illustrated weeklies had high cultural standards; reports of scandals, or pictures of nudes were excluded. But short camera-interviews about cultural affairs, art, science, theatre or politics played an important part. In 1930–31 the *Münchner Illustrierte Presse* published, with the title *Deutsche Köpfe* (German personalities) a series of photo-interviews with painters like Liebermann and Slevogt, Nobel Prize-winners like Wilhelm Ostwald, Haber, Bergius, the inventor of artificial petrol, and Max Planck, the pioneer physicist whose 'Quantum Theory' had contributed to the changed ideas we now have about the universe.

Planck was no dry scientist, and could be witty. When I met him, standing behind an old-fashioned standing-desk, wearing a black suit and with gold-rimmed spectacles on his hooked nose, he demonstrated one of his favourite joke-experiments.

'What' he asked me 'falls quicker, a five-mark coin or a small piece of paper?'

Remembering my schooldays, when I had learnt that, under ordinary conditions the resistance of the air influences free fall, I answered 'Naturally the coin will reach the ground first'.

'Wrong' said the professor 'as I will now demonstrate'.

He took a five-mark piece and put a small piece of paper on top of it, releasing the coin in a horizontal position. In overcoming the air resistance, the coin cleared the way for the piece of paper, pressed against the coin by the displaced air; both arrived together on the floor, the paper still resting on the coin.

Max Liebermann, President of the Academy and the principal Impressionist painter in Germany, lived in his parental home on the Brandenburger Tor, Pariser Platz, Unter den Linden. He liked to show visitors his important collection of French Impressionists. He would point out the essential difference between the French and German Impressionists: 'Our painters today lack enthusiasm and profound experience. For the French Impressionists, painting was not only a visual matter, but an affair of the heart—this is what is lacking among the Germans, it is cold, prosaic, studio work. The same applies to drawing. A few strokes on paper can be as nearly perfect as a painting which has been worked at for some time . . .'

His contemporary Max Slevogt was flamboyant in appearance. I met him for the first time at a reception given by the Bavarian envoy, where, in Bavarian style, only beer was served. The Bavarian legation in Berlin still existed, a relic of the time before World War I when Bavaria had been a separate kingdom. Hindenburg was the principal guest, then well over eighty, and he stayed until long after midnight, enjoying the beer and the Bavarian *Gemütlichkeit*. Slevogt was best known as a graphic artist and illustrator, and his impressionistic style was superior to the technically brilliantly executed work of Max Klinger.

1929 The Hague Conference. Dr Gustav Stresemann, Germany's Foreign Secretary, in discussion with the German Ambassador to Holland, Count Zech.

1929 At the Hague. Chancellor of the Exchequer Philip Snowden talking to the Dutch Foreign Minister.

1931 French Foreign Minister Aristide Briand. Briand, seen here with his parliamentary secretary Alexis Léger, received the 1926 Nobel Peace prize jointly with Dr Stresemann. Briand contributed greatly to improved relations between France and Germany. He and Stresemann met for the last time at The Hague conference in the autumn of 1929, Stresemann dying in October that year. Léger, under his pen name St John Perse, was awarded the Nobel Prize for literature.

1931 French Prime Minister Laval in his special train. A French delegation paid an official state visit to Berlin in 1931, the first such visit since the war of 1870. Pierre Laval invited me to travel with him and Briand (then Foreign Minister) in their special train; in those days this invitation was something extraordinary, whereas today statesmen on such visits are surrounded by journalists.

**1 Laval is greeted on arrival in Berlin
the top-hatted station-master.**

**1931 Briand and Laval at the
Berlin radio station.**

1929 Open air service in Freiburg. Monsignor Eugenio Pacelli, Papal Nuncio in Germany, celebrating Mass at a large open air service in Freiburg.

1930 Cardinal Secretary of State Pacelli in his study at the Vatican.

1930 Porta Bronza, the main entrance to the Vatican.

1938 Canterbury Cathedral. Procession in the crypt with the Dean, Hewlett Johnson.

A Day in the Life of Mussolini

The most important and fascinating photo-interview I ever did was 'A Day in the Life of Mussolini', an essay which was an absolute novelty, and which was published all over the world. When the idea was first discussed, it was generally thought that it would not be worth while, as thousands of pictures of the Duce already existed. But these were taken in rather theatrical poses, picturing the dictator as he wanted the world to see him, as a little Caesar. My plan was to show the real Mussolini, with his real face, unposed.

The Palazzo Chigi, then the official Press Office, kept me waiting in Rome for several weeks, until I obtained an interview with *Il Capo del Governo*, to discuss my proposition, which was to photograph Mussolini, in all his activities, throughout one whole day. Finally a letter arrived, which was to work like a magic wand, opening the doors of the Palazzo Venezia, the Duce's office.

'Il Capo dell'Ufficio Stampa   Roma 13 gennaio 1931
del Capo del Governo
Palazzo Chigi

Egregio Signor Man,
   In merito alla richiesta da Lei avanzata di poter essere ricevuto in udienza da S.E. il Capo del Governo, sono lieto di poterle communicare che Sua Eccellenza La vedra mercoledi, 14 corrente, alla ore 16, a Palazzo Venezia insieme con il Suo interprete.
   La presente vale come lascia-passare per Lei e per Signor Kornicker, dal portone di Palazzo Venezia sulla Piazza omogena.
   Colgo l'occasione, per inviarle, Egregio Signor Man, i miei

migliori saluti.
Ferretti

Signor Man,
presso il Signor Kornicker,
Via Bocca di Leone II,
Roma'

Accordingly we presented ourselves at the doors of the Palazzo Venezia at four o'clock the next afternoon, 14 January 1931. Two soldiers, members of the Fascist Militia, with fixed bayonets, flanked the doors. A plain-clothes man emerged, like a threatening shadow from inside the dark gateway. After examining my credentials, and the letter, he took us inside, up a few stairs, to a large iron gate which barred the way. Reaching through the lattice, the detective touched a hidden bell, which instantly brought another detective to the far side of the gate. The two guards exchanged a few words, the lattice gate opened, and we passed in, escorted by the second detective. We were led through a number of rooms dating from the Cinquecento, built under Pope Paul II, to an exceptionally splendid waiting room, where two liveried servants, with much gold embroidery, kept an eye on us. We had to wait half-an-hour, but the time passed quickly, surrounded as we were by exquisite works of art; precious ceramics from Orvieto were displayed in glass cases, sixteenth century frescoes decorated the walls, and Byzantine enamels were on view in other cases.

The Duce's Chamberlain, in a black frock coat, took us through more rooms, lavishly decorated with paintings, until we reached the ante-room, where large frescoes depicted the Labours of Hercules. Suddenly the door opened, and I stood at the threshold of a gigantic hall, of immense height, width and depth—Mussolini's study.

The hall was empty except for a huge writing-table and chair in the far corner, diagonally opposite the door; there was a map-stand, a nine-foot-high electric lamp and no other furniture in this enormous room, which measured twenty-five yards from door to desk.

I perceived the Duce. He was behind his writing table, slightly bent forward, studying some papers. He did not look up, but I felt, I was aware that he watched my entrance with a stealthy look. It takes about half a minute to cover twenty-five yards, time enough to calculate a visitor's qualities. How does he behave when walking across the highly-polished marble floor, smooth as a mirror? How greatly is he impressed by these amazing surroundings? How frightened is he by the echo of his own footsteps?

I was well-prepared for this strange reception. I entered without a trace of self-consciousness, and walked across to him in a dignified way, as suited the occasion. If the Duce was an actor, I could be one too. I was composed as the Duce gave me the Fascist salute, before shaking hands.

As a former journalist, Mussolini was intrigued by our proposition, when mapped out to him in detail. To our surprise he not only agreed that I should follow him like a shadow, taking photographs whenever I wanted, but suggested that we should start the next morning, at seven o'clock, at his official residence, the Villa Torlonia.

The Villa Torlonia was surrounded by an enormous park. I did not have to wait long for the Duce, who was in the habit of riding in this park for half-an-hour before breakfast. He showed me a few tricks he had learnt, jumping over hurdles and riding up some steps in the park, demonstrating his skill for my benefit.

By nine he was at his desk in the Palazzo Venezia, working in what I would call the most uncomfortable study in the world. We stayed with him there for three hours, while he received his private secretary, the head of his Cabinet, Terruzzi, the Commandant of the Fascist Militia, and a number of other visitors. All had to stand opposite the Duce; he only got up once, when talking to Terruzzi. During the morning, I had ample opportunity to observe him intimately, and to photograph him without poses or theatrical gestures. He never knew when I was going to take a picture, as my camera was constantly at the ready on its tripod.

Time passed very quickly. Being limited to the two-dozen plates I carried with me, I had to be careful not to waste any, taking my photographs at crucial moments and giving Mussolini no time to pose. Sometimes the camera was only three yards away from him, and I changed my position as I thought suitable.

There was an incident during the morning session of particular interest, giving a clue to Mussolini's character. His Minister of Information (*Il Segretario dell' Ufficio della Stampa*) visited him daily. Mussolini realised the importance of the press, and wanted to know what the world thought of him and of his Government. He was not satisfied with a report given to him by his Minister, and insisted on seeing for himself, being able to read German, French and English. The press chief, Ferretti, had been through a stack of foreign papers, marking passages of interest to the Duce. While Ferretti stood opposite to him, Mussolini sat at his desk, glancing through the pile. He put to one side anything that aroused his interest, for later study. Those he did not wish to retain he threw high into the air, already reading the next one, leaving Ferretti to catch the papers as they fell, like a schoolboy catching a ball.

Though all the working day was usually spent at his desk, he sometimes took time off to show himself in public, in the gardens of the Villa Borghese, riding about on horseback. He staged one of these public displays for my benefit, passing a prearranged point, after receiving a signal from the enormous number of detectives in attendance that the way was clear. The detectives had searched the public, and had nearly arrested me by mistake.

On another afternoon, he went to Ostia, the nearby seaside resort. This old Roman seaport had enjoyed his especial favour; having cleared the nearby marshes of malaria-breeding mosquitoes, Mussolini had succeeded in persuading some Romans to build summer houses there.

When Mussolini went on a trip of this kind, the head of the Secret Police had a busy day. The route to be followed was heavily guarded, and the surrounding countryside was searched, for several miles on each side, by mounted police, to make sure that there was nobody about to upset the Duce. Mussolini liked to race along the new coast road. He was followed by a trail of Secret Police in cars, who swarmed around him when he stopped.

During one of these trips, which we witnessed, a tiny incident occurred in the dunes at Ostia. Had it not been staged for my benefit, which I believe it was, it would have shown that Mussolini was greatly concerned for the welfare of the Italian people, in spite of the preoccupations he had as Head of State, and Minister of several portfolios.

We were walking along the sandy beach when we met two young fisher-boys, carrying a sack of fresh oysters and a bottle of Chianti—the latter probably being a mistake by an over-eager stage-manager. The Duce stopped the boys, ate some of the oysters, drank some Chianti from the bottle and chatted with the two ragged youths, as a democratic ruler might. He learnt that one of the boys' father, an old fisherman, was ill and had lost his licence to sell fish in Ostia market, through some trivial mishap. Mussolini gave orders for the case to be looked into favourably, and called one of his suite to give the boys 200 lire, a considerable amount at that time.

A few years later, I passed through Rome again, and tried to get another audience with Mussolini. I had no luck. Perhaps the Duce did not like my having shown his true face to the world.

1930 Palazzo Venezia, Rome. Benito Mussolini in his enormous study at the Palazzo Venezia
dagger on it, and a lectern. The wall decorations are painted.

alking to a visitor. The room is empty except for Mussolini's writing table, a small side table with a

1931 Mussolini giving orders to Terruzzi, Commandant of the Facist Militia.

1931 Mussolini, unposed, reading the daily papers.

1931 (Top) Mussolini with his press chief, Ferretti.

1931 Mussolini riding up steps in the park of the Villa Torlonia, Rome. Riding at seven in the morning was part of the daily routine.

Ruthenia under Czech rule

It is worth recording this short *intermezzo*, because of the great changes that have taken place in Eastern Europe, since World War II and the establishment of the Iron Curtain.

In 1930, Thomas Masaryk was still President of the Czechoslovak Republic. The tension which had existed between this country and Germany had eased, and I was one of the first German journalists to be allowed to visit the more remote eastern parts of the young republic. Of particular interest was the province of Ruthenia, or Carpathian Russia, as it was also called. Brown bears still roamed the forests of this region, which stretched far into the Balkans. Ruthenia, with Uzhorod as its capital, had been part of the Hungarian Monarchy, until the newly-founded Czechoslovakia added the province to its territory in 1920. Under pressure from Hitler, it was given back to Hungary in 1938, but was annexed by Russia after World War II, and then became part of the Soviet Ukraine.

In 1930 the population of Ruthenia was a mixture of different nationalities. The languages in use were Russian, Hungarian, Rumanian, Yiddish and Hebrew, and the signs were in all these tongues. One of the towns, Munkacz, was inhabited by 40,000 Orthodox Jews, and was famous for its two Wonder-Rabbis, Rabbi Spira and Rabbi Meyer-Leifer, who both had a great number of followers. The natural beauty of the province, the fascinating mixture of inhabitants, the native Huzules, in their picturesque lambswool-lined costumes with coloured embroidery, the gypsies and the Orthodox Jews in their caftans and fur-lined berets, all gave this country a special flavour.

During my stay in Munkacz, I got to know the District Overseer of this Jewish community, a man with fairly modern and enlightened views, who did not think highly of the Jewish law, which does not permit photography of people. I was keen to photograph the Jewish Prayer School, and my friend's advice proved very helpful. 'Do not speak German' he told me, 'German is very similar to Yiddish, and will be understood; so speak English and nobody will know what you are saying. You will be taken for a stranger, who does not understand the habits of the town. In any case, tomorrow is a feast day, when it is forbidden by law to give you a sound thrashing. If you just go into the Prayer School, take your photograph quickly, and go out again at once, nothing will happen to you.'

I accepted this good advice. Apart from some angry looks and threatening gestures, nothing happened to me. Through this strange religious law, I got my photograph.

1930 Carpathian Russia (Ruthenia). Sunday service in the country of the *Huzulen*, an ancient peasant tribe which lived by cattle-breeding. For this Russian Orthodox service, the peasants wore traditional costume.

1930 (Top right) Art Market Jasina. The market was held in one of the longest village streets in the world.

1930 (Right) The people of Jasina meeting in the Sunday market place.

1930 Jewish Prayer School, Munkacz.
Munkacz, in Carpathian Russia, was at this time
inhabited by about 50,000 orthodox Jews. There
was also a Prayer School known all over
Ruthenia and the Jewish Grammar School.

1930 Miracle-rabbi Meier-Leifer. There
were two miracle-rabbis in Munkacz—Spira and
Meier-Leifer. It is strictly forbidden for
orthodox Jews to have their photographs taken,
but Rabbi Meier-Leifer pretended to
misunderstand what I was doing.

1930 Outside a synagogue, Munkacz.

1930 Orthodox Jews on a feast day.

1930 Orthodox Jew sitting in the sun, Munkacz.

The Gentleman Photographer

The hotel one stays at is not without some importance; and good behaviour and a decent appearance are often a half-way step to success.

Towards the end of the Twenties, luxury hotels of the Ritz class were still exclusive. People who frequented such hotels were either of some importance, or they were imposters. It was a necessity for anyone wishing to achieve success in Vienna in those days to stay at the Old Hotel Bristol, where Edward, Prince of Wales used to stay. That is why I, too, put up at the Bristol when I visited Vienna in the autumn of 1929. I wanted to meet the leading politicians and artists. Also my liaison officer lived there permanently. This was the writer Karl Tschuppig, who had made a name for himself as a biographer of the Hapsburgs. He used to lunch off a quarter-pound of boiled ham, eaten straight out of a paper bag in his hotel bedroom; but, when he used the lift, he gave the lift-boy a silver coin.

Tschuppig knew everybody who was anybody in Vienna, not superficially, but intimately. Through him I came into contact with the Bundes-President, Miklas, with Chancellor Schober, former Chancellor Monsignor Ignaz Seipel, who lived in a monastery, and with the rather left-wing Mayor of Vienna, Seitz. I also met that strange woman Alma Mahler-Werfel, in her palatial home, where the walls were marble-lined; in the Twenties, the cream of intellectual Vienna centred around her. When I photographed this naturally dominating figure, she was married to Franz Werfel, the internationally-known writer, a tender and sensitive figure.

These were the last great days of Vienna. I met Alban Berg, the composer of *Wozzeck*, the great painter Oskar Kokoschka, the dramatist Karl Schönherr and the conductor Clemens Krauss. Katharina Schratt, once the close friend of the Emperor Franz Joseph, was still alive. I nearly succeeded in visiting and photographing her, in her house at Schönbrunn. This house was next door to the Emperor's palace, and her garden had an inconspicuous gate into the royal park, so that she could come and go without causing a scandal. Unfortunately she fell ill, and could not keep the appointment we had made. Tschuppig took a bleak view of Austria's future. 'You will see' he told me, and this was in 1929, 'this Austrian Corporal, Hitler, will never rest until he enters Vienna on a white horse.' This prophecy was fulfilled seven years later, but the white horse was a Mercedes.

Like all Viennese of standing, my friend Tschuppig spent the summer months at Bad Ischl. This was the place where the *haute volée* gathered, not only to escape from the capital in summer, but also to be near the Court. The Emperor Franz Joseph had been dead for more than ten years, but his spirit pervaded the spa; his monument, a bronze statue of him clad in hunting dress, with leather shorts and a small hat decorated with a chamois beard, stood in the park, a reminder of the 'good old days'. Blue blood ran through the veins of the visitors to this spa, in contrast to red Vienna. When the Hapsburgs held a family reunion at Bad Ischl in 1930, I also went there. No other place would have been more suitable for such a mass-meeting of Princes and Archdukes than this imperial spa.

The famous operetta-composer Franz Lehár was among those who had a summer villa at Bad Ischl. Best known for his *Merry Widow*, *Paganini*, and *The Land of Smiles*, he was a most charming and amiable elderly gentleman. In his spare time he enjoyed breeding tree-frogs, which lived in large glass containers in his sitting room.

Not only in Vienna was it decisive to choose the right hotel. Many years later, in 1949, King Bhumibol of Thailand became engaged to the most beautiful daughter of the Thai Ambassador to London, Princess Sirikit Kitiyakara; *Picture Post* asked me to get a picture story on the young royal couple. The King, then just 21, was studying in Lausanne. His flower of a Princess was attending a world-famous finishing school in Switzerland. The King, a keen racing driver, had just recovered from a serious road-accident to his sports car; he still suffered from brain and eye damage, and had to wear dark glasses.

I had a letter of introduction from the bride's father, himself a royal Prince; but Luang Prasert Maitri, a diplomat of some standing who had been educated in England, the King's Private Secretary, was most doubtful about my request to be allowed to photograph the royal couple. There were lengthy discussions, during which he learned that my assistant and I were staying at the Beau Rivage. This world-famous luxury hotel at Ouchy was one of the finest in Switzerland, and was the haunt of ex-kings and ex-queens. When he learned this, he changed his mind, and promised to put my proposal before the King. Before we left, he asked 'Are you really staying at the Beau Rivage?' I gave him the room numbers, and he promised to reply in a few days.

The very next morning, the telephone rang in my room at a very early hour: the King's Private Secretary wanted to speak to me, and was waiting in the hall. When I came down, he had nothing to tell me, only that I would have the King's decision in a few days' time. At first I could not understand why the Private Secretary had come to see me. But after some reflection, I understood—he wanted to be quite certain that we were staying at the Beau Rivage, and not just using the address, something often done in the East.

And, as staying there was synonymous with being 'somebody', I got my audience with the King and his royal bride.

From Vienna I travelled on to Hungary, then a Kingdom without a King, ruled by an Admiral without a fleet; I arrived in Budapest in October 1929. At that time the old Hungarian aristocracy still dominated the entire life of the country. Hungary was a sort of connecting link between the East and the West, in which the ordinary citizen enjoyed, compared with today, a certain freedom. The charming double-town of Budapest, separated by the Danube, united Western culture with the splendours of the Orient; wine, women and song ruled the night life in grand style. While the Rumanian capital of Bucharest, 650 kilometres to the East, orientated itself towards Paris, Budapest, still under the Hapsburg influence, looked towards Germany; German was the language of the educated classes.

While in Budapest, I learnt that the Court was to shoot, at the weekend, near the old hunting-lodge at Gödöle. Not only the Regent—Admiral Horthy—but also Archduke

Joseph and Count Bethlen were to take part in this hare and pheasant-shoot. Through Bethlen, I got an invitation.

Nothing could have illustrated better the feudal system which still existed, than this *battue*. About 200 beaters, peasants from the neighbourhood, advanced through the forest in a huge circle, making a lot of noise. Horthy, Joseph and Bethlen were standing at favoured spots, and knocked down one hare or pheasant after another. They were excellent shots, and hardly ever missed. In a couple of hours, the bag was over 50 hares and 70 pheasants.

Afterwards, breakfast followed in a forest clearing. A large table, wooden stools and even a white table cloth appeared. Camp fires were lit round about, and some of the newly-shot prey were roasted. Tokay was served, green peppers were on the table, and a small gipsy band played Hungarian melodies in the background. The beaters sat on the ground at a respectful distance, watching their masters eating and drinking.

At this elaborate and well-served meal, I sat next to the Archduke, who talked a great deal to me, and declared himself very interested in the stories of my travels. Shortly before the end of the meal, he said 'At all events, my dear Sir, I am glad that such a well-travelled man as yourself should have visited our beautiful country. Too little is known about Hungary in Western Europe.' He drained his glass of Tokay, and continued 'What does the rest of Europe know about Hungary, eh? They think of us in terms of paprika, Tokay and gipsy music . . . bah, what nonsense!'

1930 Alban Berg working on the score of Lulu at his Viennese home. Berg belonged to a group of composers including Bartok, Hindemith and Schönberg, whose pupil he was. He is best known for his opera *Wozzeck*, inspired by Büchner's tragedy.

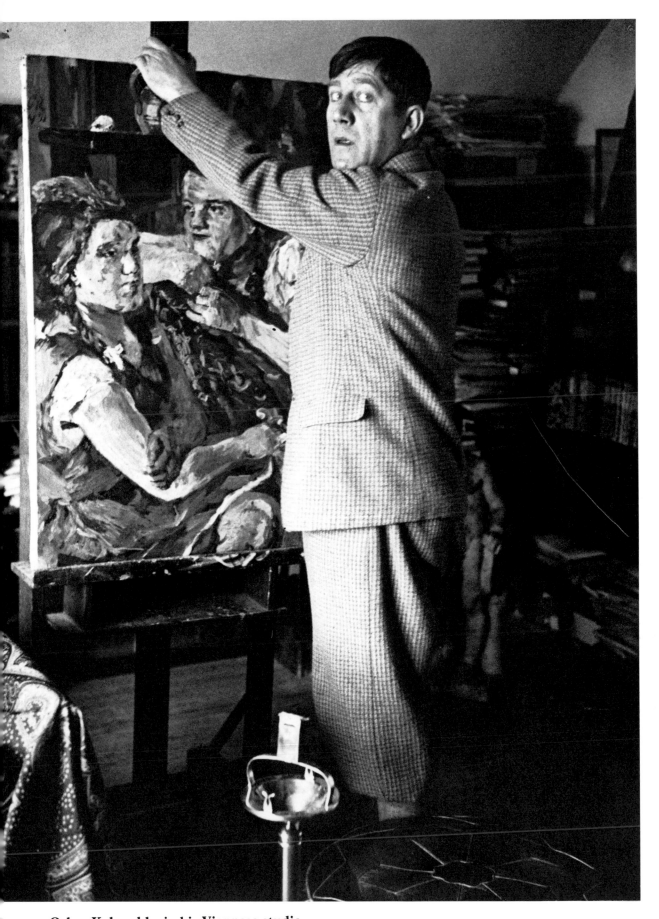

1929–30 Oskar Kokoschka in his Viennese studio.

1929 The writer Franz Werfel, with his wife Alma Mahler. Alma drew many of her famous contemporaries into her circle.

1929 Former Chancellor, Monsignor Ignatz Seipel, in Vienna. After retirement he lived in a monastery.

1929 The German writer Gerhardt Hauptmann at a rehearsal, Heidelberg Festival.

1929 Franz Lehár. Lehár conducting the first night of his operetta *The Land of Smiles*, Metropole Theatre, Berlin.

1929 The Court goes shooting. At this time
Hungary was a kingdom without a King, ruled
by an Admiral without a fleet. Feudal conditions
prevailed. When the Regent, Admiral Nikolas
von Horthy, Archduke Joseph and Count
Bethlen went shooting, their sumptuous
breakfast was served at a table in the woods,
covered with white linen. The beaters sat on the
ground round a camp fire, at a respectful distance.

1929 Regent Nikolas von Horthy.

1929 After the shooting—the bag is paraded.

1929 Beaters round the camp fire.

1932 Crossing a waterway on Hallig Hooge.

1932 Building a dyke to protect the land from the North Sea.

1930 Peasants harvesting in the German Zips (Hungary).

1931 A Lay Brother returning from work in the fields to the Benedictine Monastery, Beuron.

1932 Filippo Tommaso Marinetti, Founder of Futurism. Marinetti and friends had published the *Manifesto Futuristico* in 1909. Here the bow-tied Marinetti stands in the middle, next to the sitting Mino Somenzi, editor of the magazine *Futurismo*; On the left, Prampolini and the futurist poet Bruno G. Sanzin stand in front of a painting by Depero.

1932 Marchese Guglielmo Marconi, Senator and Nobel Prize winner, the inventor of wireless.

1932 Ottorino Respighi and his wife. The composer of chamber and orchestral music, best known perhaps for the *Fountains of Rome*.

1932 Luigi Pirandello, dramatist. Best known for *Six Characters in search of an Author*.

1932 Antonio G. Bragaglia,
the Futurist painter
in his studio.

1932 Pietro Mascagni.
The composer of *Cavalleria Rusticana* in the Hotel Plaza, Rome, where he lived permanently.

Music in Pictures

Music is primarily enjoyed through the ear, the sense of sight playing a very minor part. In most concert halls, especially if they are of vast dimensions, like the Royal Albert Hall in London, only the privileged few who sit near the platform can get visual impressions of what is happening in the orchestra; but, as a rule, they can only get a view of the conductor's back.

It was a novelty to sit, as I first did at the end of the Twenties, facing a famous conductor, at the side of a no-less-famous soloist; my camera, on its tripod, was correctly taken by the audience to be a new instrument.

The emotions evoked in the conductor by the composer's score is not only reflected in the beat of his baton, but also in his bearing and in his facial expression, normally unseen by the listener. He lifts his eyebrows, and the orchestra is reminded of the approaching *crescendo*; he closes his eyes, with a serene face, and the orchestra knows it has to play with soul and feeling. Every mood, reflected in these ways, gives the musicians the lead.

Methods of conducting are also expressions of temperament, and vary with different nationalities. Some world-famed conductors have developed the strange habit of humming or talking; some soloists do the same, and the famous pianist Edwin Fischer used to shout while performing.

Nearly every conductor has a favourite composer, in whom he specialises. In the late twenties, Furtwängler, the conductor of the Berlin Philharmonic Orchestra, was regarded as one of the most important interpreters of Beethoven, while Bruno Walter was famous for Mozart, and Toscanini, through his Bayreuth performances, for Wagner.

In the musical life of London, Sir Henry Wood, the conductor of the Promenade Concerts, was very important. These concerts, with low admission charges, were started at the Queen's Hall. When this hall was totally destroyed in the war, the concerts were transferred to the Royal Albert Hall, where up to 4000 people got acquainted with classical and modern music. Inspired by the success of the 'Proms', concerts were started at the London Museum in the Thirties—these were attended to such an extent that some of the listeners had to sit on the floor.

Though films and television have today enabled us to see in detail orchestral performances and conductors, it was quite an achievement, in the Twenties, to sweep away the prejudice against the taking of such pictures, which conquered new ground in photography.

1942 Benno Moisevitch at a London concert.

1942 Sir Henry Wood, founder of the 'Promenade Concerts', conducting in the Royal Albert Hall.
The concerts were originally held in the Queen's Hall, but moved to the Albert Hall after bombing.

1938 London Museum Concert. The audience spilled over into the galleries.

1929 Igor Stravinsky, rehearsing in Berlin.

1944 Yehudi Menuhin rehearsing.

1938 The pianist Edwin Fischer at a London Museum concert.

1930 Wilhelm Furtwängler with the Berlin Philharmonic Orchestra. Paul Hindemith
as solo viola on the right.

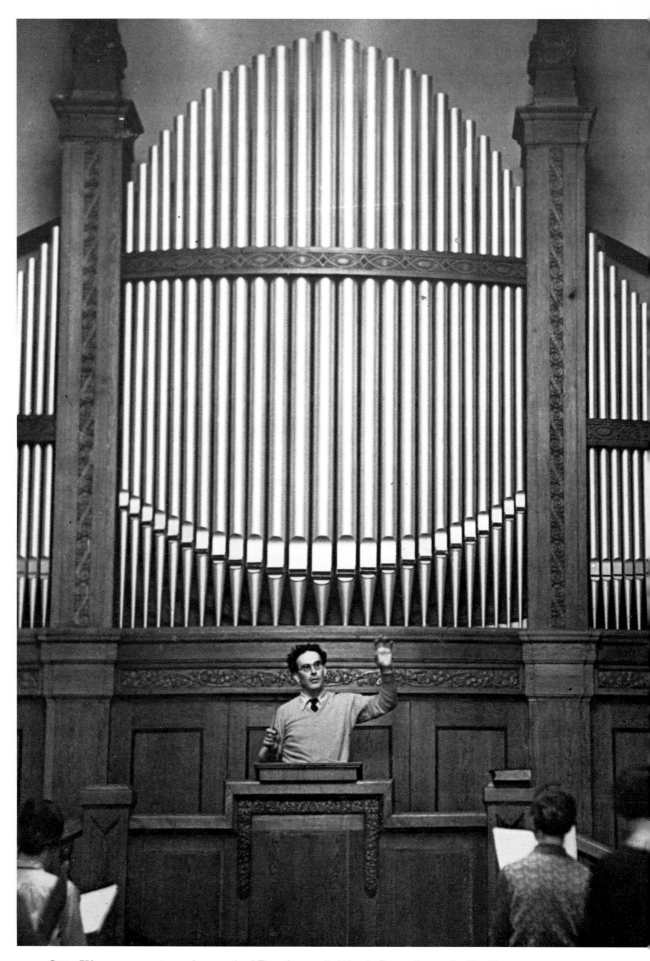

1929 Otto Klemperer at a rehearsal of Beethoven's Ninth Symphony in Berlin.

1929 Berlin Philharmonic Orchestra rehearsing.

1929 Bassoons at rehearsal.

1942 The composer Benjamin Britten.

1939 The Australian pianist Eileen Joyce.

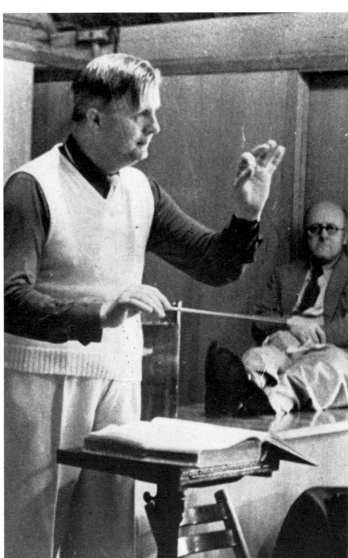

1939 **Fritz Busch conducting a rehearsal, Glyndebourne.** In the background, John Christie, the founder and owner of Glyndebourne Opera House.

1934 **The B.B.C. Symphony Orchestra's double-basses at rehearsal, Queen's Hall, London.**

1936 Sir Thomas Beecham rehearses in the
Old Queen's Hall, London.

1939 Bronislaw Huberman. Huberman, one
of the finest violin *virtuosi* of his time, played for
half an hour for my benefit, in his room in the
Hyde Park Hotel, London.

Journey to the Desert

After my big story on Mussolini, some discord developed with the editor of the *Münchner Illustrierte Presse*. I accepted a number of commissions from the *Berliner Illustrierte*. One of my most successful trips for this magazine was a visit to Libya, then an Italian colony, in December 1932.

During a short stop-over in Rome, I called on a number of people who were important in the cultural life of the capital. These included Pietro Mascagni, the composer of *Cavalleria Rusticana*, who lived permanently in a Roman hotel, surrounded by dried laurel-wreaths, mementoes of past triumphs; Marchese Guglielmo Marconi, President of the Royal Academy, in his *palazzo*, where the walls of his study were lined with antique red silk; the composer Ottorino Respighi, in his villa outside Rome; Filippo Marinetti, the father of Futurism, surrounded by his friends; the dramatist Luigi Pirandello, who was directing a rehearsal at the Teatro Argentina; the picturesque figure of the painter Bragaglia.

The next stage of my journey was Naples, the springboard for North Africa. There I called on the Russian writer Maxim Gorky. He suffered from a respiratory disease, and had special permission from Stalin to spend the winter months in the mild climate of southern Italy. He lived in a villa at Sorrento, set in a beautiful garden with tropical plants. When I called there, I was told that Gorky was ill in bed. When I pointed out that I came from the House of Ullstein, his German publishers, he asked me, through his son, to come back in the afternoon.

Gorky spoke only Russian, but his son understood German and acted as our interpreter. In spite of his serious illness, he chain-smoked *papyros*, and the atmosphere of the room was thick with smoke. Most of the time he sat behind his desk, talking constantly to me. When he got no response, he gazed at me with his fascinating pale eyes, stroking his moustache; then he would smile, realising the difficulties of our conversation, and ask his son to translate. In spite of the difficulties, I felt I was meeting a man of great distinction, from whose aura one could not escape.

Changes had been threatening in Germany for many months which, in the end, brought Hitler to power. Gorky naturally wanted to hear from me what manner of man Hitler was. I had seen Hitler in the Twenties, sitting in the open-air Hofgarten Café in Munich, holding court and eating cream buns. I had heard some of his Beercellar speeches, and had witnessed his abortive coup, when he tried to seize power in Munich, marching with Ludendorff to the Feldherren Halle. I had been present at his subsequent trial, when he was sentenced to a term of imprisonment at the fortress of Landsberg, where he wrote *Mein Kampf*, and from which he got a premature discharge. I had therefore, plenty of opportunity to form my own opinion of this Austrian Corporal. I had met the other dictator, Mussolini, a man who, if ruthless, nevertheless had a certain originality. I wondered if Gorky would be able to follow my thoughts. I was sitting opposite a genius, whose powerful intellect impressed me though I could not understand a word he said. Could this magnanimous soul understand the sinister way in which Hitler thought? Certainly he expressed satisfaction at what I was able to tell him.

The meeting lasted over an hour, and exhausted the great writer. Before he retired, he asked me to prompt Ullstein to republish his works, the current edition being out of print. He could not imagine that, in a short while, there would be no place in Nazi Germany for the books of this Russian revolutionary.

In good weather, one could fly from Naples to Tripoli in 1932. The safety record was good, and all flights were cancelled in bad weather. Therefore, in winter, one usually had to travel by boat, a three-day voyage passing Syracuse and Malta.

Libya was an Italian colony, and the port of Tripoli a prosperous town, where the surrounding desert had been made fertile by elaborate irrigation, with windmills pumping water from deep wells. Fruit and vegetables were of exquisite quality, and two grain harvests could be gathered in one year.

I set out, with my assistant, to travel, in an old Ford we had hired, to the oasis of Ghadames, 250 miles inland, on the fringe of the Sahara. After the first 50 miles, our road abruptly subsided into sandy desert. Rain was quite exceptional in this district, but there was a tropical cloudburst on our first afternoon out. The stony bed of a *wadi* we had to cross was rapidly transformed into a raging stream. Naturally there was no bridge, but our Ford was rather stork-legged, and we tried to cross the wild torrent at what we thought was a shallow ford. But the water was deeper than we supposed and it got into the engine; we broke down in the middle of the stream. Night was approaching, and the downpour was incessant. We had no choice but to strip, bundle the photographic equipment onto our heads and wade waist-deep throught the wild water, leaving the car behind.

Three hours later, we arrived, wet to the bone, at Fort Nalut, a military outpost high up in the Jebel Nefusa. We spent the night there, and the next morning the Italian Commandant sent a detachment of soldiers down to the river. The car was towed out, but the damage could not be repaired on the spot. We were able to continue our journey in a military truck.

The rain had stopped. The sky was blue and the sun burning. By the time we were deeper into the sandy desert, the terrifying *Ghibli*, the desert wind blowing from the Sudan, had become so strong that flying sand had reduced visibility to a few yards. We had to stop and spend the night in the sand dunes. In our party were a few, rather fat, Arab women, whom the Italian Government kept for the 'entertainment' of the soldiers in the lonely desert outposts. From time to time these women changed over, and this was one of the 'reliefs'. One of these corpulent women apparently regarded me as a likely victim, and followed me around until a Corporal chased her away.

By the next morning the sand-storm had died down, and we continued our journey to Fort Derge, anxiously awaited; a search party had already been sent out to look for us. An exercise of the famous Mehara Camel Corps was to take place nearby. These blond camels can move very fast, even gallop, and can cover three times as much ground as ordinary camels. I was keen to photograph the exercise but, in spite of my credentials, the Commanding Officer refused permission.

We reached our goal towards evening, when we gradually discerned the outline of the Ghadames oasis. Coming nearer we could see the palm trees swaying in the fresh evening breeze, whispering softly and making us realise why the Arabs called this place the 'magic city'. The history of the oasis went back 2000 years, perhaps more. The Garamantes, a cultured tribe described by Herodotus, lived here. Their descendants, the Tuaregs, the self-styled noblemen of the desert, now lived in the neighbourhood.

As it stood in 1932, the oasis buildings were pure eastern architecture, with walls and gates of a very early date. The women lived on the flat inter-connected roofs. No man was allowed up there, so the women were able to be unveiled. When the men left their houses, they locked the door and hung the key round their neck. They dominated the streets and squares of the old town, loafing around all day in the deep shadows, waiting for the call of the Imam from the minaret to the evening prayers.

Life here was one of contemplation, unaffected by the tempo of civilisation. There was only one clock in the town, a primitive water-clock. This was a copper pot with a small hole in the bottom. Filled with water, it took exactly three minutes to empty. Every time the watchman refilled the pot, he made a knot in a piece of palm-fibre string. As time was counted from sunrise to sunset, the watchman started his day's work at dawn.

In the world of Islam, Ghadames was a holy city. Many marabouts were buried there; saints sat motionless at street corners, deep in meditation, rosary in hand. Unaware of the outside world, one did not appreciate the passing of time when in this place. One only recalled that many miles of sandy desert had to be traversed to get there, and that these sandy wastes had to be reconquered to escape from the dream.

I was cut off from the outside world for three weeks. Back in Tripoli, I learnt the surprising news that Hitler, who had acquired German citizenship by being appointed a Government official by his Nazi friends in Braunschweig, had now become Chancellor of the Weimar Republic, appointed by Hindenburg. I went to see the German Consul in Tripoli, Schubert, whom I had contacted earlier. He was the owner of the Tripoli brewery. He explained to me in detail how von Papen and Meissner had paved the way, and induced Hindenburg to take this fatal step.

Schubert arranged for me to interview Marshal Badoglio, the Governor of Libya. I complained that the Commandant at Derge had prevented me from photographing the Mehara Camel Corps. Badoglio did not approve of this decision, and arranged for another exercise to take place at Fort Mizdah, in the desert about 200 miles inland, especially for my benefit. The commander of the Fort invited me to stay in the suite usually occupied by the Duke of Aosta; for security, a Tuareg was posted at my door.

I had a visa for Morocco, but we decided to go to Tunis, to await further developments in Germany. The only connection was by boat. Before leaving Tripoli, I called at the French Consulate, where no objections were raised. We planned to save time by leaving the boat at Sousse, travelling on to Tunis by rail. We left the boat without any problem but, while buying tickets at the station, I was tapped on the shoulder. Turning round I was faced with two plain-clothes policemen, who arrested us on the charge of having entered the country illegally. The general exodus from Germany had started, and the French authorities were already suspicious of anyone travelling with German papers. We were escorted back to the boat; to prevent us from escaping two men were posted at the foot of the gangway until the steamer left the next morning. A wire sent to the German Consul at Tunis smoothed away this difficulty; the Consul came to the port on our arrival, arranged a courtesy visit to the

Resident-General, and subsequently obtained a visa.

In 1933 Tunisia was a strictly Mohammedan country; it was impossible for unbelievers to enter mosques, except in Kairuan, and women were veiled to the eyes in public. For one day in every week, the cemetery was reserved for women and their young children. No man was allowed in, and the women walked about unveiled, picnicking on the gravestones, and enjoying the sunshine on their pale faces, the fresh air and the natural beauties of the place. A high wall protected them from peeping toms. I had been warned to avoid this strange spectacle, as a religious law was involved. But my curiosity was aroused. I searched along the wall, and found a place where I could get a glimpse over the top, but enough for a picture using a long-focus lens. The women and children sitting about playing and lunching off the grave-stones made an enjoyable photograph. It was a risky enterprise, but well worth while. Now the picture is an historical document of the past; since independence, the strict religious laws of Tunisia have been abolished.

1932 Berber with flint and tinder for lighting.

1932 A caravan coming home at sunset, Tripoli, Libya.

1932 **A gate in the 2000-year-old oasis of Ghadames.** The Tuaregs, desert nomads, occasionally visit the oasis.

1932 In the oasis of Ghadames, Libya. The women of Ghadames live on the roofs of the interconnected houses; the men are not allowed on the roofs as the women are unveiled. For the greater part of the day, the men sit lazily in the shadows in the streets until the muezzin calls them to prayer.

1932 The town walls, Tripoli at sunset.

1932 An Arab giving the fascist salute. (Left, above) At this time, Libya was an Italian colony under Mussolini.

1932 An ancient water-clock. (Far left) In Ghadames time stands still, and there was no modern clock. Time was kept by a small copper vessel, from which water drained through a small hole. Each time the vessel emptied itself, the man made a knot in a piece of string, so measuring the time.

1932 Negro girl carrying water. (Left) Her father was still a slave.

1933 Cemetery in Tunis. On one day each week the cemetery was closed to men; only women were allowed in, taking off their veils and picnicking on the graves.

1932 Mehara Camel-
Corps in the Libyan
Desert.

1933 Picnic on a grave-
stone, Tunis cemetery.

1932 Maxim Gorky. The writer suffered from lung trouble, and had special permission from Stalin to spend the winter months in the mild climate of Sorrento, Southern Italy.

1936 The Russian cellist Piatigorski during a London concert.

Going North

When I am asked what, in my career, has made the greatest impact on me, I find it very difficult to give a precise answer. I have met so many of the great men of our time—statesmen, scientists, writers, artists—that I am unable to decide who has impressed me most.

I was always very fond of travelling. Aged eighteen, I travelled alone by boat from Bremerhaven to Genoa, calling at Antwerp, Gibraltar and Algiers. The fourteen-day trip, in a 45,000-ton passenger liner on its way to the Far East, cost only 100 marks, then five pounds sterling, travelling third class, all alone in a four-berth cabin, and landing in every country visited without the need of a passport. My journey into the Libyan desert more than 50 years ago was certainly one of my greatest adventures, only to be compared with my journey to the Canadian north in 1933.

Back in Berlin in March 1933, I found a completely changed country. The Nazis were in control, press censorship had been established and a number of friends, mainly journalists and writers, had already been arrested. Though some of the editors at the House of Ullstein were still at their desks, it was clear to me that Goebbels, with his new laws, would make it impossible to go on working for the press in Germany without blowing the Nazi propaganda trumpet.

Thinking this over, I told Ullstein's Illustration Director, Szafranski, that I could only continue as a contributor outside Germany, where I would not come into conflict with the Nazis. I suggested that I should go on a world tour, starting in Canada, then quite an undeveloped country, and continuing across the Pacific to Japan, and so on. This plan was accepted, and financial arrangements were made. Before I left, this trusting man—a Jew—assured me that nothing could happen to the House of Ullstein because, he said 'We are on excellent terms with Herr Goebbels, the Propaganda Minister.' I replied by telling him 'I can promise you that in six months time you will no longer be sitting in your editorial chair.' Having crossed Canada from east to west, and from south up to the Arctic circle, travelling on dog-sleighs across the frozen Hudson's Bay, and enduring temperatures of 45 degrees centigrade below zero, a message reached me at the distant outpost of Churchill Harbour that the House of Ullstein had been completely disowned by the Nazis, the leading directors dismissed and replaced by party members. I was recalled from my world tour, after seven months in Canada.

Canada is a vast country, bigger than the United States. From the inland port of Montreal, one has to travel well over 3000 miles westwards to reach Vancouver on the Pacific Coast. In my day this took three days and four nights by transcontinental train. These trains were the only means of communication as flying was not yet generally introduced, and the journey by road could only be achieved by crossing several times into the United States. The distance from south to north is similar. In 1933, only a small belt of land along the American border, about 200 miles in extent, was properly populated and opened up to traffic.

The northern province of Canada attracted me more than anything else. The North-West Territories, with its enormous forests and wilderness, was not at that time even mapped completely. There were no roads at all, as neither the Alaska nor the Mackenzie Highways had been built. The virgin forest and dense brushwood were impenetrable. Travel was either by canoe or boat on the many rivers and lakes, or by single-engined hydroplane. This vast province, 1,300,000 square miles in extent, was then inhabited by about 3000 Indians, 200 Eskimos and 1500 white men. To reach Great Bear Lake, in the Arctic circle, I travelled by Fairchild monoplane. The journey took about twelve hours, with two stops for refuelling, flying at about 800 feet, giving a splendid view of the country.

Our destination, Cameron Bay, on Great Bear Lake, comprised a handful of primitive log cabins. These were inhabited by the few people who worked in the pitch-blende and silver mines, and by some prospectors, who used the place as the base for their explorations. Life was hard, and men had to be powerful to endure the solitude. They had to be self-reliant, and use their physical strength every day to conquer the challenge of nature. But the lonely natural surroundings were beautiful, and the nights with the crackling Northern Lights were exciting for the newcomer.

Tinned food flown in by the small aeroplanes formed the staple diet, supplemented by enormous lake trout. Even at midsummer the topsoil only thawed for about three inches, so that nothing could be grown locally. To transport the minerals, a small twenty-foot schooner had been built from local timber, powered by a diesel motor laboriously flown in from the south.

To begin with, the weather was fair, and quite warm in the day. I used the time to inspect the mines. After a full moon, the weather turned rough and cold. I had intended to return south by water, and it suited me quite well when the captain of the little schooner, the *Speed*, who was in fact in charge of the whole enterprise, suggested that we should leave the same evening. With him at the wheel, he hoped to cover the 250 miles across Great Bear Lake to Fort Franklin in about 30 hours. We started out, gliding peacefully across the placid lake in what was to turn out to be the most eventful part of my Canadian trip.

By European standards, everything on the American continent is enormous. This vast lake is about half as large again as Wales. By the time we were out of sight of the shore, the little vessel started to heave about considerably. We unrolled our sleeping bags in the hold, amid the penetrating smell from the diesel oil drums. When I awoke in the middle of the night, I noticed two members of the crew making tea on a small gasoline cooker. The whole boat was filled with fumes, and these Indians were refilling the cooker from an open jug of gasoline drawn from one of the drums.

When I mentioned this to the captain the next morning, he replied 'I know. I have often told the boys to be more careful. But what can I do? They must have their tea. Besides we won't blow up.' 'A fatalistic hope' I replied. 'You would take the same attitude if you had lived in the north for ten years' was his reply.

It was hard to realise how these huge lakes could produce ocean-sized waves, breaking over the deck. Our little vessel was tossed about like a nut-shell. The captain got worried and decided to seek shelter in a small bay. We anchored near Grizzly Bear Mountain, and went ashore. Although only September, it had become bitterly cold. The first snow had fallen on the mountains; we sheltered in our sleeping bags in tents which the Indians put up. For five days, waiting for the weather to settle down, we explored the neighbouring bush. Probably no human being had ever set foot ashore at this point. We wandered on virgin land; and when our food began to run short we shot duck and ptarmigan, which the Indians roasted on big open fires. Once, forcing our way through a mixture of brushwood, dwarf birches and small fir trees, we stumbled on a family of brown bears, the mother and three cubs sitting in the branches of a tree, while the old father kept guard on the ground below. Eventually the weather cleared, and we packed up our camp and carried on to Fort Franklin, where our cargo was transferred to several river canoes, for the journey down the rapids of the Bear River, a tributary of the mighty Mackenzie River, to Fort Norman.

The Hudson's Bay Company was then running an old paddle-steamer, the *Distributor*, on the Mackenzie River, between Aklavik and Fort Smith. This old-fashioned vessel was log-burning. Every day the boat had to stop to refuel from piles of logs stacked along the route in preparation. The trip I joined at Fort Norman, the last of the season before the big freeze-up, did not proceed without hold-ups. We had to cross the Great Slave Lake, and stormy weather there held us up for a week, until the lake was calm enough for our antique craft to make the crossing. I did not reach Edmonton until the end of September. When I read the *Edmonton Journal*, I found the following on the front page:

Two Men Dead, Five Others Stranded, After Explosion On Schooner in Far North

(Canadian Press Despatch.)

Edmonton, Nov. 10. — With two companions dead and two others safe at Cameron Bay, five men were stranded Thursday night on the bleak shores of Great Bear lake following an explosion aboard a schooner and the wreck of a barge on the rocky shores.

Fatally burned when an explosion caused fire and destroyed the schooner, "Speed," of the Northern Waterways service, Harry Jebb, engineer, and Jimmy Potts, a helper, are dead. Stan Hooker and Bill Parker were in Cameron Bay after plodding through wilderness for six days. Vic Ingraham and four unidentified companions were stranded on the lake shore.

Northern radio pathways carried the news of the tragedy Thursday and an airplane was sent from Cameron Bay in an attempt to rescue the stranded men from privation and cold. It swept away from the northland base but last night no word of success or failure of its mission had reached here.

Efforts to refuel the gas schooner, "Speed," from tanks carried on the barge while the lake was choppy caused the explosion aboard the schooner which took the lives of Jebb and Potts. Ingraham and an unidentified companion made their escape from the schooner in a rubber life boat after failure to find Jebb and Potts.

Fearing destruction of the barge by fire and loss of life of all aboard, the craft was cut free from the burning "Speed." It drifted seven miles to shore and was wrecked when large waves pitched it against the rocks.

The schooner, with the barge in tow, set out October 20 from Frank-

lin for the northwest shore of Great Bear lake. When it did not arrive at Cameron Bay, October 31, when they were six days overdue, investigations were started. A plane piloted by Harry Hayters failed to find any trace of the boats or men.

Wednesday Hooker and Parker reached Cameron Bay after walking six days. They were two of the five men aboard the barge. Leaving their three companions who survived the wreck of the barge and the two survivors from the schooner on the Great Bear lake shore, they set out to get aid. Weary and suffering from exposure, they reached Cameron Bay as more extensive plans for the search were being made.

With a doctor and medical supplies aboard, another plane was sent from here Thursday after directions as to the finding of the five stranded men had been obtained from Hooker and Parker. No word is expected from the plane until today.

When I told people in Winnipeg that I intended travelling by dog-sleigh over the ice of Hudson's Bay, they told me 'You will freeze to death in the coldest place in Canada'. To withstand the cold, I dressed like an Eskimo. The Hudson's Bay Company supplied me with an Eskimo parka and trousers, both made of caribou fur. I had high sealskin boots with soft fur soles; the frozen snow and the ice are perfectly dry, and these boots prevented the feet from getting stiff. It is amazing how the body can adapt itself to extreme conditions, if properly equipped; we were even able to sleep in our eider-down sleeping bags in a tent in the open, with the temperature outside at 45 degrees centigrade below zero.

Taking photographs in these conditions was not easy. To operate the Leica, I had to remove my fur mittens and act quickly. The small amount of oil in the camera soon froze, so that one could only take a couple of pictures before it was necessary to replace the camera under the fur parka, to be warmed by body-heat. For my Nettel-camera, I had made a box with a hot-water-bottle, but again my picture taking was limited to only a few exposures.

The whole of Hudson's Bay was an enormous landscape of ice. Travel by dog-sleigh was the only possible means of transport. At this time of the year, only trappers and their wives lived in the Arctic region, setting their traps to catch silver foxes, polar foxes and minks. These trappers lived in primitive wooden huts, patrolling their trapping lines set out in the brushwood once or twice a week to collect the wretched animals, frozen to death in the traps. For food, they shot duck and other wild birds, living a hard life in the frozen wastes. In the spring, they took their furs to sell at one of the Hudson's Bay stores, and replenished their food supplies.

We set out from Churchill, a new town on the shores of Hudson's Bay. In 1933 this place hardly existed on the map. In reality, it consisted of a railway station, a small port, a grain silo, a small radio station and a bank in a wooden barrack proudly named 'Bank of Montreal'. The railway ran from Winnipeg, and was built for the export of grain to Europe; the northern route to Liverpool was much shorter, but the port could only operate for five months in the summer.

1933 Red Indian Totem Poles. Totem poles in the Kispayaks Indian reserve, Prince Rupert district, British Columbia. These were erected in memory of the dead, with carvings by the Indians to keep evil spirits away.

1933 Great Bear Lake, North-West Territories, Canada. Arrival at Great Bear Lake at midnight. Small Fairchild monoplanes were the only link between this region in the Arctic circle and civilisation nearly 700 miles to the south. Hydroplanes were used, as landing was only possible on the numerous lakes and waterways in the north.

1933 Cameron Bay, Great Bear Lake. The mining town consisted of primitive log buildings.

1933 Cameron Bay airport.

1933 A brown bear in the North-West Territories.

1933 Red Indians of the North. Working in the mines in the North, some of the few Indians not living in reservations.

1933 Camp fire on the shores of Great Bear Lake.

1933 Dog team crossing Hudson's Bay at 45C below zero.

1933 Polar fox eating ptarmigan. Trappers and prospectors were the only inhabitants of the far North.

1933 Building an igloo in northern Canada. In Eskimo style, nights are spent, in northern Canada, in an igloo, a round hut built of blocks of frozen snow, cut with a special knife.

1933 Felix H. Man in Eskimo clothes.

1933 A trapper's log hut in the frozen North.

1933 Broken-into deep snow.

1933 Churchill Harbour, Hudson's Bay. Ships are frozen in here for six months.

1933 Montreal Harbour. An ocean-going steamer discharges grain at the great inland harbour on the St Lawrence r

England in the Thirties

After my Canadian journey, I returned to Berlin to wind up my commitments with the House of Ullstein. It had by now become law that all leading journalists had to join the *Reichspressekammer*, a Nazi organisation. At the same time working connections with Jews were forbidden, and the concentration camps were waiting for those who disobeyed these edicts. In this new German Reich, nobody was free to go abroad—an exit-permit in the form of a special stamp in your passport was required. An old acquaintance of mine, so no Nazi, had not scrupled to move from his job on a small illustrated paper to a better position on the *Illustrierte Beobachter*, the official Nazi illustrated paper. Even so, out of loyalty to me, he wrote a certificate to say that I was to go to England for him, and this certificate secured me the essential exit-permit.

I left Germany for good in May 1934. I had to leave everything behind me and travelled with only a small suitcase, to avoid suspicion. I had been told that the best way into England was by Calais and Dover. Passport control took place on the boat, during the crossing. 'How long are you going to stay in England' asked the Immigration Officer. When I replied that this depended on my work for various continental papers, my passport was stamped with an oval stamp, with the words 'Leave to land at Dover this day, 31 May 1934, on condition that the holder does not enter any employment paid or unpaid while in the United Kingdom'.

Though I thought about myself as an immigrant, legally I was only a visitor to the United Kingdom, and the oval stamp only gave me the right to stay for three months. As a journalist I could do free-lance work, even working for an English paper, provided I was not employed and paid a fixed salary or retainer, but paid separately for each job. The Immigration Officer had told me that, to extend my stay in England beyond the three months I had been given, I had to report to the Aliens Office in Bow Street for a decision. For the moment, however, I was glad to be in London, and tried not to worry about the future.

As for so many newcomers, my life in London started in Bloomsbury, in Tavistock Square, at that time with Georgian houses surrounding the green square, now all demolished. A few days after my arrival I met, by sheer accident, my old friend Stefan Lorant, the Hungarian former editor of the *Münchner Illustrierte*; he had been imprisoned soon after Hitler's take-over, but released through pressure from the Hungarian Parliament. 'You are exactly the man I would most have liked to meet at this moment' he exclaimed 'I need you, as I am planning a new weekly illustrated paper with Odhams Press.' Neither of us had known of the other's presence in London before we met. For years we had worked together in Germany, he as editor, I as his principal contributor. We were a team, complementing each other. Was it coincidence, or fate?

At that time, photo-journalism did not exist in England. The continental method of writing essays with a camera was unknown, and there were no illustrated weeklies of the continental type. The world's first illustrated paper, *The Illustrated London News*, published news photographs, pictures taken by scientists or explorers, or photographs of prominent society people. The daily press, though realising the value of photographs, worked on the principle that the first picture to reach the news desk was the best. For this reason the photographer who was the quickest, and who had the bodily strength to secure and defend the best positions, was regarded as the best. There is of course some truth in this, because the best picture can be worthless if it arrives after the paper has gone to press.

The professional press photographers of those days still used whole-plate or half-plate cameras with glass plates. Messengers on motor-cycles rushed the exposed plates from the event to the darkroom. They were developed as rapidly as possible, fixed, superficially watered, put still wet into the enlarger and made into 8″ × 10″ prints. The print, quickly washed and dipped into spirit for a moment, was dried over an open gas flame, a better method than using any of the mechanical driers of the day. The whole process was so well organised that only a matter of minutes and seconds lay between the arrival of the negative and the finished print being laid on the editor's desk.

To understand the importance of speed, it has to be remembered that English papers have several editions and that these editions, especially those of the evening papers, follow events in words and pictures. Newspapers and agencies were masters of organisation, as no means then existed for transmitting photographs by wire. Exclusive pictures of important events could be worth hundreds of pounds. It was worth-while for a big agency to hire a plane to fly back negatives, processed on the flight, of significant events on the Continent; the Associated Press did this on June 14 1934, when Hitler and Mussolini met for the first time at Venice airport, so that the picture could be in the London evening papers the same day.

Weeklies had other problems. Press-day had to be met, and a certain topicality preserved, but now the camera had to enter fields hitherto unknown, unobserved and therefore neglected. The background became as important as the main event. Photographs had to speak for themselves, captions and text playing a minor part. This conception, already five years old on the continent, was entirely new in England.

Soon after his arrival in England in May 1934, Stefan Lorant had learnt that Odhams Press were planning a reorganisation of some of their magazines. He made contact with the management, and suggested that they should publish a new illustrated weekly of the continental type. Odhams agreed, and their dying magazine *Clarion* was incorporated—in small type—with the new magazine, *Weekly Illustrated*.

Though Lorant was to be at the helm of this new paper, with me as his close collaborator, Odhams did not appoint him editor, but named Maurice Cowan, who also ran *Picturegoer*, for this post. Tom Hopkinson, then a *Clarion* writer, joined the paper as caption-writer, and assistant to Lorant, whose English was not yet fluent. James Jarché, a *Daily Mail* photographer, moved over to the new paper. Both of them were facing photo-journalism for the first time.

The preparatory dummy was put together by Lorant in June 1934, in the continental manner, using a number of my old picture-stories. As time was short, I started, that month, to produce photo-essays for the new paper. When the first number of *Weekly Illustrated* came out on July 7 1934, the bulk of the picture stories were mine; Lorant had laid out, on the usual two pages each, four photo-essays of mine. I had worked on my own, as usual, with a personal assistant, also providing the facts for the captions and the brief texts. I was paid according to the number of pages of my work which were published; for several months the paper was largely dependent on my work, and I was earning from it between £40 and £50 a week. This naturally caused some jealousy from others on the paper. Maurice Cowan, thinking after a few months that he knew how to run such a paper, plotted how to get rid of Lorant and myself.

I was overworked, and my permit to stay in England was due to expire at the end of August. I decided to take a continental holiday, leaving about eight stories behind, to be used in my absence. Lorant only hesitantly accepted my suggestion that a German friend Hübschmann should take over in my absence; the latter and I agreed that he would fade away on my return. Later on Kurt Hübschmann changed his name to Hutton.

When I returned to Dover in October, the Immigration Officer again used the oval stamp, giving me another three months in England. In the meantime the squabbles at *Weekly Illustrated* were mounting. Lorant, fighting to retain his own position, was not able to give me sufficient support. A month after my return, I left the paper, predicting to Lorant that he too would be leaving within a couple of months, a correct forecast as it turned out. *Weekly Illustrated* stumbled on without its founding fathers, until killed off by the overwhelming success of *Picture Post* in 1938; it was then reborn as *Illustrated*.

Until today, the importance of *Weekly Illustrated* as a picture magazine has yet to be assessed. It was through this paper that photo-journalism was introduced into England. When Henry Luce was preparing the publication of *Life*, he came to England to study the back issues of *Weekly Illustrated*.

After this unpleasant ending to my time with *Weekly Illustrated*, I free-lanced for various Swiss, Danish and Dutch papers. Things became somewhat difficult. I was still without a work permit; and, not being a Jew, no Woburn House supported me.

There was only one daily paper which was interested in pictures other than news-pictures or the Royal Photographic Society style. This was the *Daily Mirror*, then a daily picture paper with several editions. The editor was Cecil King, who understood the importance of pictorial messages.

In the autumn of 1935, a friend arranged for me to join the staff of the *Mirror*, on trial at first, but permanently after two weeks, at a salary of £15 a week, then the highest Fleet Street photographer's wage. My colleagues at the *Mirror* were most charming people, keenly interested in photo-journalism. They were already using Leica and Contax cameras, an exceptional thing at this date for newspaper photographers. All my photographs while with the *Daily Mirror* were published under the pseudonym 'Lensman', as were those of another very gifted contributor. This was Humphrey Spender, brother of the poet Stephen Spender, a painter who in later years was to work occasionally for *Picture Post*. Lancelot Vining, then working at the *Mirror*'s lay-out desk, only started as a contributor after I had left.

But throughout my time with the *Mirror* I was sitting on a volcano. The management had undertaken to settle the work-permit question with the Home Office. Many months passed, and though the *Mirror* emphasised that I was doing a job which no English photographer could do, and in spite of my repeated requests, the much-needed permit was not forthcoming. The situation was critical as, if my illegal activities had been discovered, I could have been deported as an unwanted alien.

I left the *Mirror* and free-lanced again for a short period. As a stills photographer at Elstree Film Studios, I was paid £10 a day. I did some portrait photography. I photographed some picture stories which an agent tried to sell to papers like *Everybody's* and *Today*, which was an abortive attempt by Newnes to start a new weekly. There were days when I was terribly hard up, and I began to feel that there was no market in England for my type of photography.

In 1937 Bernard Shaw had finally given permission to Gabriel Pascal to film his famous play *Pygmalion*. When shooting was to start at Pinewood Studios, there was a celebration lunch party, to which I managed to get an invitation. I was sitting quite near to Shaw, who was flanked by Wendy Hiller, the star of the film, and the irresistible Lady Asquith. He quietly listened to the numerous speeches, by the director Anthony Asquith, the male star Leslie Howard, and many others. All these people praised each other, and distributed advance laurels, except to the dramatist, whose name was not mentioned. Shaw waited for a moment of silence, eyeing this self-satisfied assembly with a malicious twinkle. Then he rose to his feet, a glass of water in his hand, and addressed the guests in a serious tone. 'Ladies and Gentlemen' he began 'numerous speeches in connection with the film have been made at this baptismal luncheon, and different speakers have congratulated each other in a lavish and exuberant manner. But nobody has thought of toasting the author, so I will do it myself and drink to the well-being of George Bernard Shaw.' When Shaw raised his glass of water, all stood up to join him, and Lady Asquith embraced him.

Shaw had a pungent wit. I had my first encounter with him earlier, while working for *Weekly Illustrated*. A new Shaw play was a big event in the London theatre. In 1934 rehearsals for *A Village Wooing* were taking place at the Little Theatre, in absolute secrecy, all the more so as the dramatist was also the producer. He flatly refused a request to photograph a rehearsal. But the theatre manager, knowing the value of advance publicity, had different ideas; while a rehearsal was in progress, and the house in darkness, he smuggled me into a corner seat in the front row. Shaw was not far away, at his producer's desk. I sat motionless in my corner seat, until Shaw halted the proceedings and mounted the stage to demonstrate how a scene should be played. Once or twice he interrupted his discourse to peer into the darkened house, but he could not quite see me against the glare of the footlights; but he must have heard the clicks of my camera. Suddenly he said to one of the actors 'Move your chair to the left, or people sitting in the corner of the stalls—about where this strange intruder is sitting—will not see you. This does not matter for the moment as he has not paid for his seat, but at the performance people will have paid and will want to see properly.'

I sat motionless for a while, Not knowing what to do. But his secretary appeared to say 'Mr Shaw asks you to leave the theatre, and will not continue rehearsing while you are here.' I left rapidly with my negatives, feeling that my first brush with Shaw had been quite successful.

More than 15 years later, I met Shaw again at his house at Ayot St Lawrence, where he was watching a rehearsal of his latest play *Buoyant Billions* with great interest. At ninety-three he was of exceptional mental vigour. His snow-white hair and beard framed his pink face, which was quite unlined; only his dried-up hands gave away his age. From time to time he gave some advice to the producer. The leading part was played by an actress who had never before appeared in a serious play. When she told Shaw that she had never read any of his plays, he replied 'Much better, as you come to your task fresh and unbiased.' When she asked him how to play a love-scene, he replied 'Exactly as no two finger-prints are alike, so all love-scenes are different—but *you* surely know this!'

Another of the interesting meetings which I had in the mid-thirties was with the Emperor Haile Selassie, the lion of Judah, who made good use of his time as an exile in England. When he was driven out of his country by the Italians under Mussolini, he went to live in Bath. He was very keen to study new things, not available in his own country, something that would be useful to him later on, when he returned to his throne.

When he travelled in England, there were no formalities. I often saw him on Platform 1 at Paddington Station, waiting for the Bath train. Fleet Street ignored him, but the Station Master would appear each time, in his top hat, to pay the respect due to an Emperor.

One hot Sunday in the summer of 1937 I travelled on one of the familiar red London buses to Roehampton to spend the day at an open-air swimming-pool; as usual I had a camera with me. Open-air pools of this kind were something quite new in the English capital; it was comfortable and elegant, with terraces for sun-bathing in deck-chairs, refreshments available, and was surrounded by thickly-wooded country.

When an attendant started to rope off part of the tea-terrace, I asked him what was happening. 'The Emperor of Abyssinia is coming' he replied with a grin. At first I thought he was pulling my leg. An Emperor on a Sunday afternoon, with no formality—an Imperial Majesty among the English beauties in their bikinis—I could hardly believe it!

Without any ceremony, the Lion of Judah appeared, in a half-length black cape decorated with red braid, his retinue at a respectful distance. He had a charming smile for all the pretty girls, and moved around, clearly impressed by the elegance of the new swimming pool.

Political kidnapping had yet to be invented.

By this time my passport had expired because I refused to go to the German Embassy to get it renewed. As a correspondent for continental papers, London was my domicile, and my presence had been regularised with the Aliens Department in Bow Street. One of my main connections at this time was with the *Züricher Illustrierte*, a progressive Swiss magazine.

I kept in close contact with my old friend and colleague, Stefan Lorant. When in the mid-thirties, he started to publish a magazine of his own, the pocket magazine *Lilliput*, it was only natural that I become a contributor at once. In about June 1938, Lorant sold *Lilliput*, for what was then a substantial sum, to Hulton Press, and then entered into negotiations with this young but financially very sound publishing house, about starting a weekly illustrated paper on the continental model. The new enterprise, to be called *Picture Post*, was due to start in October 1938, so there was little time for preparations.

The dummy that Lorant had made up, to persuade the advertisers and the publishers, was partly made from old pictures of mine, demonstrating the type and the style of the proposed contents. I was asked to start work at once, and travelled to Cornwall at the beginning of August to work on a number of stories. I also did some work in London, where I photographed a surgical operation for the first time in London, the 'Proms', London at night, and a five-page story on 'Life in an English village'.

Almost half the pictures in the first issue of *Picture Post* were mine. The same was true of the second issue, and even more true of the fourth. I had as usual worked with a personal assistant only. The influx of writers had not yet begun at *Picture Post*; at this time there were only Lionel Birch and Honor Balfour, from the *Oxford Mail*, both friends of mine.

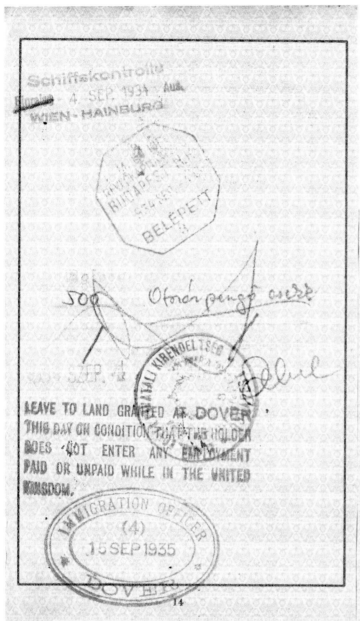

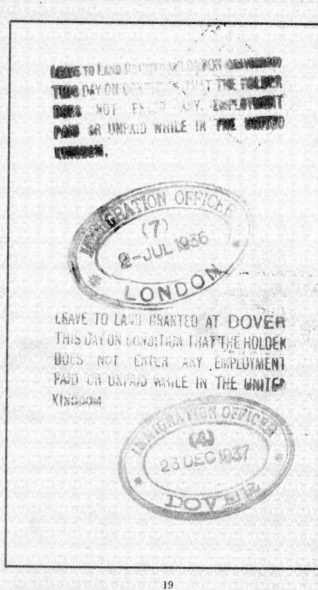

1934 Passport. In the thirties there was strict control of entry into Britain, especially as the exodus from Hitler's Germany had begun. Without a Home Office permit, you could enter the country only as a tourist, and your passport was stamped 'Leave to land granted at Dover this day on condition that the holder does not enter any employment paid or unpaid while in the United Kingdom'. As a tourist you could stay up to three months.

"How Would You Hold Hands?"
Douglas Fairbanks, jun., and Gertrude Lawrence discuss an important point of production with Miss Clemence Dane, authoress of the new play "Here Lies Truth."

"HERE LIES TRUTH"

All playgoers have enjoyed the performances of Gertrude Lawrence. Most of them have seen at least a moving reproduction of Douglas Fairbanks, jun. But so far few of us have had the chance of looking at both at the same time.

That opportunity will come to Londoners on September 19, when Miss Clemence Dane's new play, "Here Lies Truth," comes to a Shaftesbury Avenue Theatre, after a preliminary tour in the provincial theatres.

Miss Dane enjoyed considerable success with the famous "A Bill of Divorcement" and "Will Shakespeare."

Between Scenes
Gertrude Lawrence snatches a moment to see how her stage make-up is keeping pace with her emotions.

★

" That's My Cue!"
"I can never remember that bit," says Douglas Fairbanks. "It's all so different from "Catherine the Great.""

(In centre of page)
Miss Clemence Dane takes a stall for the rehearsal of her own new play, "Here Lies Truth." Miss Dane is producing the play herself.

★

(Above)
Rehearsals are often long and tiring. Gertrude Lawrence is glad that this one's come to an end.

★

(On left)
Gertrude Lawrence and Douglas Fairbanks have been great friends for several years, but they have never before appeared together on the London stage.

" Don't Go Just Yet . . ."
Gertrude Lawrence and Douglas Fairbanks, jun., rehearsing for the play "Here Lies Truth," which was originally to be known as "Moonlight is Silver." It looks as if it would have been an appropriate title.

Printed in Great Britain and Published . . . ODHAMS PRESS . . . Long Acre, W.C.2 . . . Advertisement Department . . . Long Acre, W.C.2 . . . Editorial Offices, 93 Long Acre, W.C.2 . . . Telephone : Temple Bar 2468 . . . Registered at the G.P.O. as a Newspaper.

1934 Rehearsals for Here Lies Truth. The leading players were Gertrude Lawrence and Douglas Fairbanks, Jnr; the playwright, Clemence Dane. A page from *Weekly Illustrated*, September 8th 1934.

1934 Victoria Station, London. Taxis were available on the platform to the traveller arriving at Victoria from the Continent

(Top, right) **1934 Piccadilly Circus at noon.**
Traffic was not controlled by traffic lights, and
pedestrians could cross the streets at any point.

(Right) **1934 Piccadilly Circus by night.**
Although known as 'The Centre of the World',
Piccadilly Circus was modestly lit, in spite
of the advertising, compared with today. This
photograph needed an exposure of a $\frac{1}{4}$–second
and a tripod.

1934 Shaftesbury Avenue, the heart of theatre-land, London. The theatres are out and the elegant world in tails and fur coats moves on to a restaurant for dinner.

1934 Children in the West End. Poor children, on their own could be seen at night in the fashionable districts, eagerly watching the rich passing by.

1934 Hansom Cab in Regent Street. It was still possible at this date to use a Hansom Cab instead of a taxi.

1934 Piccadilly Circus at night. Late editions and the next morning's papers were on sale at night at Piccadilly Circus. The 'lady' is on the look-out for a customer.

1934 Night street scene. Peanuts and roasted chestnuts were on sale in the streets.

1934 Charing Cross Road the street of booksellers at night. In the thirties you could still make discoveries in the second-hand book shops.

1934 Noontide fog, London. Thick fog, known as pea-soup, was frequent in the thirties. Daylight faded, the traffic grew lame, and visibility sometimes shrank to three yards.

1934 Chamber Music in Chelsea. A concert in an elegant private house was a festive occasion, with the guests in dinner jackets and evening dresses. The members of this quintet are, from the left, A. Hobday, Adela Fachieri, Alexander Fachieri, the well-known Spanish cellist Gaspar Cassado and the English violinist Jelly d'Aragny.

1934 Chamber Music in Chelsea. Guests listen to the music in a handsome drawing-room.

1934 'La Argentina'. One of the most famous Spanish dancers of her day photographed during an actual performance from a box in the grand tier.

1936 Acrobatic Dancers, Windmill Theatre, London. In those days, this act was thought to be risqué.

1936 Outside Covent Garden Opera House during an interval.

1934 Theatre Queue, Shaftesbury Avenue. It was necessary to queue for the cheaper theatre seats, using folding camp-stool. Buskers and musicians entertained the queue.

1934 British Museum Reading Room. The famous library of the British Museum is one of the largest in the world, with millions of printed books and thousands of manuscripts, dating back to Greek, Roman and Egyptian times. All books are available to Reading Room card-holders, for study in the circular Reading Room; they may not be taken out, have to be returned every evening, but may be reserved for further study.

1934 Playwright and novelist J. B. Priestley at home, Isle of Wight.

1934 Elisabeth Bergner at home, Hampstead. One of the most successful actresses in Germany in the twenties, Elisabeth Bergner appeared several times on the London stage, after her immigration to England in 1934.

1934–5 Palace Pier, Brighton. An hour's journey from London, Brighton was a favourite seaside resort, with entertainments of all sorts.

1934 Café on the Pier, Brighton. The long pier, built on pylons, was a masterpiece of Victorian steel construction.

1934 Sunday afternoon, Brighton beach. Sunshade, newspapers and provisions—a pleasant day on the stony beach at Brighton.

1934 Undisturbed by the neighbours, Brighton beach.

1938 A tramp in Sussex. 'A tramp is an unemployed by profession.'

1949 Blackpool, the holiday centre for the north of England.

1949 Benches on the sea-front, Blackpool.

1949 Travelling circus, Blackpool.

1949 Spring comes to Blackpool beach.

1936 Kensington Gardens, London. Before World War II, families would spend the afternoon in Kensington Gardens on the grass. A family excursion, with the father pushing the pram, sandwiches, fresh air and sunshine in the park—before the motor car took over.

1936 In the East End, London. Most coloured people lived in the East End, where the only playground was the street.

1936 In the East End, London. The home-made carriage was primitive but useful—pedal-cars were unknown for the poorer classes.

1936 Mission in London's East End. Coloured people were looked after at Missions, where there were billiards and tea-rooms.

1936 The Lord Chancellor, the First Viscount Hailsham. The Lord Chancellor is the highest judicial official, and chairman of the House of Lords.

1934 Judges and messenger boy in London. Before World War II, wigged and gowned Judges could be seen in the streets near the Law Courts in The Strand.

1936 Bookshop window, The Temple. A second-hand barrister's wig and wig-box offered for 30 shillings.

1938 Pub in Edgware Road, London. The pub, with its different bars, played an important part in English social life.

1938 Outside the pub, children waiting for their parents. Only open at certain hours, children were not admitted, and waited outside for their parents, sometimes until late in the evening.

34 Epsom Derby. The Derby is the most important 'classic' race of the year; it is attended by all classes, a kind of people's festival.

1937 G. B. Shaw on the Pygmalion set, his first film.

Shaw on stage. G. B. S. rehearsing 'A Village Wooing' at the Little Theatre.

1934 Jack Hylton and his band. In the thirties Jack Hylton's band was one of the best in England, giving concerts which filled an evening.

1938 Making dresses for a Revue. (Top, right) Between the wars, Charles Cochran was the leading English impresario in the field of revue. His 'Young Ladies' were both beautiful and well trained; décor and costumes were designed and made in special work-shops.

1935 Rumba, often performed on stage.

1943 Queen Elizabeth, now the Queen Mother, at a charity function.

37 King George VI and his Queen, Opening of Parliament. At the start of a new Session of Parliament, the King ~~~ds a Speech from the Throne, outlining a programme worked out by the Prime Minister. On the way to this act ~~~ State, the splendid State Coach is used, with footmen and 'Beefeaters' in attendance.

Picture Post

When the first number of *Picture Post* went to press, trenches were being dug in Hyde Park to protect the civil population against air raids. In contrast to this fatuous improvised protection, the first issue of the paper, which was intended to conquer England in a quick assault, was well prepared. This issue, of 750,000 copies, was sold out and had to be reprinted. By the spring, the circulation was nearly 1.4 million. Meanwhile Chamberlain had been and gone to Munich, the clouds of war had receded, the race for re-arming was on, and the economy was prospering.

Many experts had forecast that a new picture paper could not succeed. Was not the fate of *Weekly Illustrated* proof enough? Conditions in England were said to be completely different from the continent, and everything was against such a venture. The large editions of the Sunday papers would, it was said, leave no room for an illustrated weekly. Their large organisations and printing facilities enabled them to change words and pictures up to the very last moment; this was something that *Picture Post* would never be able to do, as this would involve changing a whole photogravure cylinder, covering sixteen pages, a long and costly business.

The phenomenal success of *Picture Post* made nonsense of all these predictions. Why, then, was the weekly such a smashing success? There were a number of causes, but the most important of these lay in the conception and direction of the paper. Stefan Lorant, the editor, and the two principal contributors, Hutton and myself, were all experienced in our fields. We had mastered our jobs and worked together as a team. Tom Hopkinson, the assistant editor, had learnt a lot in four years with *Weekly Illustrated*. His main job was to oversee the 'words' part of the weekly, while Lorant as editor and picture-expert held his protective hand over the whole project. The British public was, for the first time, introduced to abundant well-composed large-scale picture essays about ordinary, everyday things, which people were familiar with, but had never consciously observed.

The photographs had been taken in a fresh and natural way, at the 'fruitful moment' without any posing. The lay-out showed a new and bold approach. Each number brought something new, and there was always a great variety of themes. Although *Picture Post* catered for everybody, it would be wrong to call it a family paper, as it appealed to the more sophisticated reader, but the magazine could be left about and read by children. Sex and crime were excluded, such cheap methods of attracting readers being left for a later generation.

In issue number one, published on October 1 1938, there were 80 pages for what was even then a ridiculously low price of three pence. There were 39 pages of pictures, 22 of reading matter, and a four-page colour supplement on great British painters. The buyer needed several hours to go through the magazine thoroughly.

Music, sport, surgery, village life, dog-races, glamour girls, bohemian London, the self-governing island of Sark, Chelsea pensioners, the birth of a cartoon, showing the popular cartoonist Low at work, London at night, a horse auction at Tattersalls, the Spanish Civil War, future Tories, the London County Council at work—these were a few of the themes, which always provided something for everyone. The reading matter, based on thorough research, and written by experts, dealt thoroughly, over six or seven pages, with such topics as The Press, The Post Office, The B.B.C., and so on.

In the earliest days, *Picture Post* had no strong political standpoint. It was certainly anti-Nazi, and issue nine had a piece called 'Back to the Middle Ages' on Nazi cruelties. Equal space was given to the Liberal, Labour and Conservative Party Congresses. Edward Hulton, the proprietor, reserved a page each week for his own article, where he developed his personal views on such subjects as race-relations, the Pope, Hitler, Spain, the Treaty of Versailles; he tended to stick to world affairs and avoid party politics.

In later years the character of *Picture Post* was to change somewhat. A leftish attitude emerged during the second half of World War II. Long articles by eminent writers criticised the government and the conduct of the war; there was much about post-war Britain. Though originally a picture paper, *Picture Post* was attempting to play a decisive part in politics.

By December 1938, the paper had grown to over 100 pages. Articles on provincial towns and cities started to appear, to widen the interest in the paper. *Picture Post* was firmly established, and the circulation grew steadily, although the advertising did not greatly increase until the New Year, when new advertising budgets came into operation.

Unlike *Weekly Illustrated*, where Stefan Lorant had been anonymous, he was now named as editor on the contents page. But the names of the two photo-journalists who contributed so much to the success of the paper were never mentioned; all the work was anonymous, so that the public were not to know that the backbone of the paper consisted of foreigners. Although I still had no work-permit, and all my contributions were on a free-lance basis, Lorant had designated me 'Chief Photographer of *Picture Post*'.

Unlike the German weekly illustrated papers, where essays or interviews were limited to two or three pages, *Picture Post* spread important pieces over six, even eight, pages. The accompanying text had to be much more detailed, so a number of journalists were taken onto the staff. Coming from a different branch of journalism, they tried to dominate the photographers. As I resisted these attempts, I was not very popular with the journalists; I insisted that, when on a job, photographers came first, as we were, after all, an illustrated paper.

When on a story, I was already visualising the final layout. I always discussed each project with the editor beforehand, and therefore knew what space he intended to give to the story. I never took rolls of film, but selected a handful of the best negatives for enlargement. As soon as I had pressed the shutter, I knew how the picture would be used, and I only took about the number of pictures required, a habit formed in the old glass-plate days. If I was working with Macdonald Hastings, a friend who worked well with me as he fully understood my methods, I would often say, having taken a picture 'Mac, that will be our half-page picture.'

Towards the end of World War II, I started to work with a personal assistant, who later travelled with me all over Europe, and to the West Indies and America. She not only collected the facts, which would form the basis of the covering article which we would later write together, but would smooth the way when meeting the famous. John Masefield once said to her 'I see that your job is to make the victim look charming.' Later, she was to become my wife.

Before the war, it was the custom to take photographs in theatres at what were called photocalls. Certain scenes were posed, special lighting was introduced, and the stiff and unnatural pictures that resulted were used for publicity purposes. In Germany I had taken photographs during actual performances or final rehearsals, which meant photographs at crucial moments in natural lighting conditions. I introduced this method to the English stage. As it was never troublesome, I was often admitted to theatres closed to other photographers. I acquired an intimate knowledge of directors and actors. On one occasion, at a rehearsal which dragged on till midnight, John Gielgud, who was directing a Shakespeare play, banged a sword on the proscenium arch and shouted 'I want everybody to leave the theatre at once, as I do not wish anyone to see me losing my temper.' But I was allowed to stay, with my assistant.

As I was the only one who could manage to achieve this type of photograph, I took all the theatre pictures for *Picture Post*; this had the great advantage that there were always tickets available to me for new plays. Much the same applied to the ballet, where the International Ballet used me to photograph all their ballets, for display and publicity.

The leading political figure before, and at the beginning of, World War II was the Prime Minister, Neville Chamberlain. When he returned from his meeting with Hitler at Munich in 1938, did he really believe that 'Peace in our time' was secured by the famous piece of paper he waved at Croydon Airport? Or was it his intention to gain time for Britain, then largely unprepared, to re-arm?

Many Members of Parliament, of both right and left, were of the opinion, at the time of Munich, that relations with Soviet Russia had been neglected, and that this vast country should no longer be cold-shouldered. Since the Soviet Embassy had been established in London, no Prime Minister had crossed its threshold. The first approach was made when a trade delegation visited Moscow. Soon after this, in the spring of 1939, the Soviet Ambassador in London, Ivan Maisky, gave an evening reception at the Embassy in 'Millionaires Row'. Chamberlain attended this historic occasion.

It was a gala event, with tailcoats and decorations. In the presence of the Diplomatic Corps, Cabinet Ministers, and distinguished people from science the arts and society, the Prime Minister had a long talk with the Ambassador. People like H. G. Wells, J. B. Priestley, Lord Horder and Lord Samuel, the Liberal leader, thronged the rich cold buffet. Russian champagne from the Crimea and vodka were the favourite drinks, and the 450 guests consumed more than twenty pounds of caviar. In the hall a larger-than-life portrait of Stalin looked benignly down on this illustrious gathering, so full of consequence for the future. Representing *Picture Post*, I was the only photo-journalist present, dressed by Moss Bros, as I had had to leave my tail-coat behind in Germany.

A couple of weeks before the war started, I found a cottage in the Chilterns with vacant possession; anticipating what was going to happen, I installed myself there at once. 'The Old Forge', my eighteenth-century cottage, was at Flaunden, a small hamlet of about 20 houses, with a church, a pub and the Flaunden General Stores, a tiny shop where cigarettes and postage stamps could be bought.

On the first Sunday of the war, a beautiful, sunny day, the church bells suddenly sounded the alarm. An elderly woman, the village air-raid-warden, with a gas-mask fixed over her face, shouted through the mask 'Keep indoors, enemy aeroplanes are coming.' But nothing came; and the Phoney War lasted for some time.

The fear of the enemy within, the fifth column, caused me problems. As my time in Canada counted towards residence in Britain, I had been in a position to apply for naturalisation six months before the war broke out. My case was under investigation, but the outbreak of war stopped all naturalisation. I had become friendly with Sir Stafford Cripps, who tried to get me into the Ministry of Information. But no alien could be employed at the Ministry; as the Home Office ruled that naturalisation could only be granted to aliens already working for a Ministry, it was a vicious circle. 'Enemy Aliens' such as myself had to go before a tribunal. Before this took place, I could not travel more than six miles from my home. I could cycle the four miles into Watford, where the *Picture Post* offices had moved to, but my contributions stopped. The tribunal classified me as 'A', meaning friendly alien, after my dear friend Honor Balfour had spoken up for me. This classification meant that I could travel all over Britain, be out of doors until midnight, and continue my work for *Picture Post*. Certain restricted areas were taboo, and I could not photograph anything military or in any way connected with the war.

The Phoney War came to a sudden end in the late spring of 1940. Hitler had overrun Holland and Belgium and burst round the Maginot Line. It looked grim for England. Although the bulk of the British Army were miraculously evacuated from Dunkirk, they had to leave their weapons behind. Invasion threatened.

A few days before these events, I had met Sir Stafford Cripps by chance at the Marble Arch Corner House, where he was eating his usual salad lunch. I told him that some of my friends had been arrested; he did not think that this would be my fate, but I was to ring him up if anything went wrong—but when things did go wrong, Cripps had left London to become British Ambassador in Moscow.

It happened on another beautiful Sunday morning, in June 1940. Paris had fallen; Mussolini, thinking he might be too late to share the booty, had declared war on the Allies. I was planting flowers in my garden at Flaunden, when the peaceful silence was broken by five men coming through my garden gate, four of them in uniform. The other said 'I must arrest you' and posted the uniformed men around the cottage to prevent any attempt to escape. This man, the Police Superintendent from Hemel Hempstead, gave me half-an-hour to get some things together, and then took me off to a single cell in Bedford Prison.

The authorities had lost their heads. Aliens were arrested as they walked along the streets. The Superintendent probably thought that, if he arrested all the aliens in his district, he would certainly have rounded up all the Nazis, if there happened to be any. He had managed to collect a fair number in this way, and after a few days, we were taken by train to Euston, and then marched across London under military escort to Victoria Station, heartily abused by those we passed on the way, who supposed that we were dangerous spies. Hampton Court Race Course was the assembly-point for thousands of internees, and we were all cross-examined there. The MI5 Colonel who interviewed me at once realised that a mistake had been made. He told me 'I cannot help you at present, but I can give you some advice. Be persistent in your efforts to get out. Try everything, and you will eventually succeed.'

He was right. Three months later I was free, back at Flaunden and working again for *Picture Post*. But the Police Superintendent evidently regarded me as a dangerous person still. One day I looked out of an upstairs window of the cottage and noticed somebody hidden in the bushes opposite. I went down and found the village policeman lying in the ditch. He was very embarrassed at being discovered. I said 'I am not going out today so you are waiting in vain—you had better go home.'

Stefan Lorant, though not interned, had suffered from a number of restrictions, one of the reasons why he had given up his position and emigrated to the United States in July, while I was interned. Tom Hopkinson had taken over as editor.

Many firms, evacuated at the beginning of the war from central London, came back to London during the Phoney War, when nothing much happened. This included *Picture Post*, which then stayed throughout the 'Blitz' and the rest of the war. Many buildings between Fleet Street and Holborn Circus were destroyed, but Fleet Street itself, and the Evening Standard building in Shoe Lane, which housed *Picture Post*, survived, although a large bomb once went right through the building without exploding.

At the time of the 'Blitz', in the autumn of 1940, when London was assaulted nightly, most offices closed about 3.30 to enable people to leave before the attacks began. Regularly at twilight, the ear-splitting sirens sounded. Those not fortunate enough to have found a place in the country to stay at, moved off to the shelters, and to the tube stations deep underground. My cottage was full, with people sleeping in the cellar, in the barn at the bottom of the garden, and in the old forge.

One of these friends had a car in which we used to travel to London and back. Soon after 4, we used to meet at a café in Baker Street. The sirens had sounded by the time we reached Hendon. At night we could see, from the garden, the gruesome and deadly firework display over central London. And when we came in to London the next morning, the ruins and devastation of the night's work often blocked the way. Coming from the peace of the English countryside made war seem utterly senseless. Walls came down but work went on. After the Luftwaffe's enormous losses, the bombing attacks stopped, and business in the City and Fleet Street returned to normal. There were occasional small raids, but they made little impact.

Hitler's 'Secret Weapon', the V1 Flying bomb, was a different matter. This unpleasant missile, then a complete novelty, was designed not only to cause destruction, but also to undermine the morale of the ordinary citizens who, as Hitler already knew, were not cowed easily. The flying bomb was a ghastly thing. While its noisy and gradual approach gave some warning, the growling noise of the missile coming nearer and nearer, getting louder and louder, grated on one's nerves, as it was impossible to predict where the thing would come down and explode.

It soon became clear that the upper stories of buildings were the most vulnerable, while the ground floors and basements were comparatively safe, especially those on the west and north aspects. Large offices and stores had roof-spotters, and an internal warning system to be used if the building was in the line of fire and danger threatened. At *Picture Post* we had such a system, and when the office warning sounded, nearly all the staff would rush down to the basement.

One morning we were having our weekly editorial meeting. The entire editorial staff was assembled, discussing the paper to go to press the following week, when the familiar noise of an approaching flying bomb could be heard. The conference was taking place in the editor's room on the top floor, with glass partitions all round. Although our discussion was a lively one, the humming noise of the approaching bomb could be heard, *crescendo*. I had just suggested a 'Holiday in London' story—something much encouraged by the Government at this time to prevent unnecessary travel—when the office alarm went off a second time.

But nobody in the room made the slightest move, and Tom Hopkinson continued his conference, apparently quite unmoved. The noise grew louder and louder until one could feel the vibration of the engine. Then it cut out. We expected a crash at any moment, perhaps blowing us all into eternity together. Nobody moved. There was a deathly silence, and one could hear one's neighbour breathing. What a display of British bravery, I thought. Even though I thought I was entitled to dive under the desk, not having had the training of an English public school, I could not do so.

The huge crash came seconds later. The bomb had gone off at the bottom of Kingsway, about 400 yards away. We now rushed out into the street. A large cloud of small pieces of paper floated overhead, some settling down in Shoe Lane. I picked some up; they were all cheques, filled in and signed. A bank had been hit.

These weekly editorial conferences were most important. It is no easy task to go on producing, week after week, a paper of quality, attractive to a wide circle of readers. Many suggestions were made at these weekly meetings, and all could have their say about the suggestions, but the editor had the last word. A number of ideas for stories, good and bad, came from letters from readers. Some were mere curiosities, such as a model of the Houses of Parliament made from lard, but others were useful, opening new fields, to be discussed and investigated.

Even the simple happenings of everyday life could be rewarding if freshly depicted with open eyes. One simple opportunity I had was based on observation. When a big building was going up in London, with a lot of machinery involved, people of all types stopped to peer through a peep-hole in the fence surrounding the building-site. A study of the various faces and the different expressions furnished the material for a most successful series of pictures.

On another occasion I took fifteen pictures at an open-air swimming pool, twelve of which were used to illustrate the essence of the pool, from the beauty stretched out in the sun in her bikini, to the man with the R.A.F. moustache skimming the surface of the water like a sea-lion.

My connection with *Picture Post* opened many doors for me; I had by this means the opportunity of meeting some of the Heads of State who had sought refuge in the United Kingdom, when driven out of their own countries by Hitler.

Edouard Beneš, the President of Czechoslovakia, had his headquarters at a country house in Buckinghamshire, not too far from London, where he presided over his Government-in-exile. In fine weather, the President liked to sit at a small table on the well-kept lawn in front of this manor house, in the shade of an old copper-beech. Beautiful trees, such as can only be found in English parks, surrounded the lawn, bordering a small wood. On this lawn Beneš received members of his Cabinet and other visitors, and dictated letters to his secretary.

When he was called to the telephone in the house, I made use of the time by looking round the garden, and ventured to the edge of the wood to photograph the house and garden. But I quickly turned back; behind every third or fourth tree was a Czech soldier with a rifle.

King Haakon of Norway needed no such protection, and moved freely about London during his exile. There was a considerable Norwegian colony in London, and the Norwegian merchant fleet was very active on the Allies' side. The King, who was related to the English

Royal Family, had an aversion to photographers, as he had once been photographed in a tactless manner at a moment of great emotion, and blinded by a flash-light. It was not easy to get him to agree to my presence at a party given by Admiral Lord Evans in honour of General Smuts, the Prime Minister of South Africa. But the King finally yielded and, having noticed my restrained behaviour, even allowed me, a few days later, to photograph him at a meeting of his Cabinet at the Norwegian Embassy—something very unusual more than 30 years ago.

The Duchy of Luxemburg, the small country between Germany and France, though declared neutral, had to face occupation in both World Wars. In World War II the Grand-Ducal family fled to England, escaping from the Nazis. But the monarchy survived all storms. The Grand Duchess Adelheid had a democratic attitude. She allowed me to be present at a meeting of her Cabinet, and I noticed the great skill she displayed when conducting her affairs of state. After the Cabinet meeting, she received me privately, with the Prince Consort, her son Jean, the present Grand-Duke, and her two daughters; it was a picture of pleasant harmony, in sad circumstances, without any formality.

King Zog of Albania, after being deposed by Mussolini, lived for some time at the Ritz Hotel, with his Queen, formally a Hungarian Countess, and insisted much more rigorously on his royal dignity. He demanded that an old-fashioned group should be built up around himself, sitting in a large chair, as if on a throne. He was surrounded by his numerous sisters, who shared his exile, and some of his Ministers were told to complete the group by standing at a reverential distance in the background. It was exactly like a Court photograph of 50 years earlier. In the end I was able to persuade him to be taken sitting at his desk, in a most elegant tailored suit; but he never took his eyes off the camera.

During the war years, England was divided into two zones—the ordinary one, and the restricted zone, from which I, like other aliens, was banned. All military installations were also taboo, and one day, when I took a photograph of a military band giving a concert in Hyde Park, I was tapped on the shoulder and told 'Don't you know that you must not photograph a military object?'

Having been classified as a friendly alien I could continue my work with *Picture Post*, but the idea of a 'fifth column' prevailed and a question was even asked in the House of Commons 'Is the Home Secretary aware that an enemy alien goes in and out the various ministries.'

Many great actors and actresses, John Gielgud, Leslie Henson, Vivien Leigh and Beatrice Lillie among them, were in a group which from time to time entertained at big bomber stations when there was no flying. *Picture Post* wanted me to photograph such a show, but the Chief Constable of the area refused me permission to enter the airfield. However the Station Commander, Wing-Commander Edwards, V.C., took a different view and invited me as a personal guest; he sent his own car to collect me, and I travelled to the bomber station in company with the Security Officer. The Chief Constable could not object to this arrangement. I was able to take my pictures, and had a most enjoyable evening afterwards; never have I consumed so much whisky as I did on that occasion.

As the war went on, *Picture Post* got thinner and thinner as the paper shortage got more and more severe. Stories which had previously been spread over four or six pages were now restricted to two or three. War pictures took up more and more of the available space. In consequence my earnings, still based on the extent of my contributions, and still at the original rates, dropped considerably. I had to look for work outside *Picture Post*, and I ventured into a new sphere when I accepted assignments for *Harper's Bazaar*. I introduced a style of fashion photography, new then, but in wide use to this day. Naturally I had to show dresses and materials to their best advantage; my photographs were not studio-stills, but were full of life, taken in action, without posing and in natural surroundings.

While I was, on the one hand, very glad to have been able to continue working during the war, apart from one short interruption, it has to be said, on the other hand, that the Hulton Press had taken full advantage of the fact that I was an alien in a foreign country. I had to accept what was offered me, hand over all my negatives—something I had never done before—and accept payment below my usual rate. Meanwhile the publishing house and the paper were flourishing, and the proprietor was able to turn Hulton Press into a public company, at great profit. I was determined not to continue in this way, and refused to accept a new contract similar to the old one. So, when the war was over, and after seven years, I left *Picture Post*.

Through a friend, I got into contact with the George Newnes publishing house, who were showing some interest in launching a new illustrated weekly. After some discussion with the management, I suggested to Macdonald Hastings that he and I should be joint editors of the proposed magazine, he looking after the literary side of the venture, with me controlling the pictures. Newnes accepted this plan, and we both signed contracts on this basis. While preparatory work was going on, Newnes asked us to modernise the venerable *Strand Magazine*, and bring it up to date. However it turned out, after several months work, that continued paper rationing would prevent the appearance of the new weekly. The project consequently foundered, and our contracts were terminated, with appropriate compensation.

For the next few years, I was not attached to any paper, and indeed took very few photographs; my interest switched to a different sphere, in a sense going back to my early days as a student of painting and the history of art. It was from this background that I had first stumbled, as it were, into photography.

In Munich, in 1913, I had come across the work of Klee and Kandinsky at the *Galerie Goltz*. Even then I wanted to own works by artists, and bought a few drawings; but I soon realised that my means would not allow me to buy drawings of quality, and I switched to buying prints at auctions and from small dealers. I became a collector, in a modest way. A true collector does not collect without a specific aim, and limits himself to that aim. When I reflected that the youngest of the graphic arts, lithography, was invented by Aloys Senefelder as late as 1798, my goal was fixed: I would build up a collection of lithographs, from the date of its inception until the present day.

In those days, of course, it was possible to pick up masterpieces of lithography for next to nothing, as the importance of this form of graphic art was as yet unrecognised generally. Yet, as only a handful of artists, such as Constable, Turner and Monet, had not turned to lithography at some time in their careers, the collection would form a history of nineteenth and twentieth century art in miniature.

I now conceived the idea of a book on the history of lithography. Only Pennell's, published in 1898, existed, and I spent many months scrutinising the print collection in the British Museum.

This most pleasant occupation was interrupted in the autumn of 1948. *Picture Post* had again started to publish a four-page colour section every week. I was asked if I would be willing to take some colour pictures for the magazine, since the Editor was not satisfied with what he was getting from the *Picture Post* staff. The management accepted the terms I put forward, and this approach led to two years of happy co-operation with Tom Hopkinson.

Apart from a trial in 1933, I had taken no colour pictures. I was, however, confident that I could handle the technical aspects satisfactorily, and adapt my black-and-white style to colour, while my training as a painter gave me a feel for it. It was late September; so I went off at once for a month's working holiday in the south of France. When I returned to London in October, I already had some colour stories, which were duly published in *Picture Post*. Amongst these was a Matisse story; I had visited the artist at Vence, taking my first indoor colour photographs in natural surroundings, including a picture of Matisse at his easel which is recognised to this day.

From then on, I did not look back. I travelled all over Europe, collecting colour essays, and usually adding some black-and-white pictures as well. I tried everything, and found no task too difficult, even those things which it seemed must be impossible to photograph on 35mm Kodachrome. Something never done before was a sunset at Whistler's Corner in London, in December 1948, with all the glowing colour in the sky and water, Another picture not attempted before was a Canonisation in St Peter's, Rome, with Pope Pius XII.

I met many important people in my travels, such as Vincent Auriol, the President of France at the Elysée and at Rambouillet, the King of Thailand in Lausanne, President Gronchi of Italy at the Quirinale, and Martin Heidegger, the philosopher, at his Black Forest hide-away. It was comparatively easy to meet the Heads of State, as everything was arranged through diplomatic channels; it was much more difficult to photograph Heidegger. He lived at Freiburg i.B.; when I called at his house, a woman answered my ring. When I asked for Heidegger, she replied 'I am Frau Professor Heidegger. My husband is not here. He is in his cabin in the Black Forest.' When I said that I had come to photograph him, and was prepared to go up to the Black Forest to do so, she said 'I can tell you that it would be quite useless; he will never allow you to photograph him.' When I explained that I was determined to pay her husband a visit, she said 'If you are really going, would you be good enough to take a basket of vegetables, some mail and some newspapers with you? He has hardly anything to eat up there.' I agreed gladly, as this would give me an opening; it was 1949, and food was still in short supply in Germany.

When I got to the isolated retreat at Todtnauberg, I knocked at the door, saying 'I am messenger, postman and greengrocer at the same time', handing over the basket. I revealed my true purpose when I was inside, whereupon he said 'But did my wife not tell you that I never do such things?'

During the ensuing conversation, I told him that I had met all the finest European artists, and showed him some pictures of Braque, with whom I knew he was friendly. Eventually he yielded, and I took some photographs of him at his desk, wearing a white nightcap, with a French philosopher friend. When we moved outside to take some more pictures, he changed to a black night-cap. But as soon as I returned to London, I received a letter from his wife, with a request that the photographs should not be published.

In 1950 I went on a journey several months to the West Indies and to British Guiana. *Picture Post* planned a colour feature about conditions in these colonies, and about the election of the first Parliament in Trinidad. My relationship with Tom Hopkinson had been most friendly, and this last period of co-operation had been very fruitful. It was now about to come to a sudden end. When I reached the Myrtle Bank Hotel in Kingston, Jamaica, amongst the mail waiting for me was one from the Editor:

London, November 8, 1950

My dear Hans—

When you receive this letter, I will no longer be editor of *Picture Post* as I have been relieved of my post by Edward Hulton. We had an argument about a story with photographs which our men in Korea had sent back, which I wanted to publish, and which Hulton rejected . . .

I have talked to my successor, Ted Castle, and he wishes you to continue your journey as planned, to Cuba and Florida . . .

He will write to you himself . . .

All the best wishes to you both,

Yours, Tom

I was completely stunned. This was the beginning of the end. I had left London early in October. The editor and I had such a good understanding, that we had not troubled to renew my contract, due to expire in November when I would be travelling in Jamaica. Throughout the journey I had assumed that it would automatically be renewed.

The new editor, later to become Lord Castle, had other ideas. When I returned to London in January, my retainer was stopped, and I was told 'We don't need your work from this journey, as we are going to stop publishing in colour.' I would not accept this treatment, and went to Court to fight it. I had to wait two years before the case was heard in the High Court. After five days, I won a substantial sum in damages, and costs, and it was pleasant to hear Mr Justice Streatfeild say 'It was obvious that the plaintiff was a man of the utmost skill as a photographer, and he was described as the best colour photographer in the country.' The *Times* published a full report of the case. Hulton Press did not appeal.

No paper can stand losing its experienced editor and its experienced contributors at the same moment, as well as trying to change the form and style of the magazine at the same time. Playing down to the masses does not always pay. Though *Picture Post* lingered on for another six years, under a variety of editors, it was its old self only in name. It had none of the convincing vigour of the early years; one could sense sickness and death approaching. The increased importance of television may have had something to do with it, but other magazines managed to survive, and even flourish, for many years. The right people in the right place could have overcome the difficulties; but they had been sacked, for which the publishers had to pay a heavy price.

While waiting for the Court hearing, I had done some special colour work for *Life* and for *Sports Illustrated*. In London, Heinemann had published *Eight European Artists*, a book of my photographs, in colour and black-and-white showing Europe's most important artists at work, at leisure and at home. It was a true documentary presentation of these artists, unusually published with three languages in one volume, and with original hand-written contributions by each artist, as well as a drawing of each. At much the same time Heinemann also published my *150 Years of Artists' Lithography*, the result of my extensive studies in the British Museum.

Later on, during the Fifties, I became a regular contributor to the *Sunday Times*. I had a difficult task, as the editor wanted a photograph on Friday evenings which would be sufficiently topical to use on the front page on Sunday. If the picture turned out to be insufficiently topical, it was used on an inside page. I gave up this assignment after a year.

1937 G. B. S. drinks his own health in water.

1939 Earl Winterton, 'Father' of the House of Commons. As an Irish peer he was able to sit in the House of Commons.

1942 David Lloyd George, Liberal Statesman, British Prime Minister 1916–22, at home at Churt.

1939 Sir William Beveridge. Beveridge was author of the Beveridge Plan of 1942, which greatly influenced post-war social policies.

1939 Neville Chamberlain, Prime Minister, with Ambassador Maisky. 'Peace in our time' Chamberlain had announced on his return from visiting Hitler in Munich in 1938. But this peace was not built on solid foundations, and the British Government started to approach Soviet Russia, to try to avoid danger from that direction. For the first time a British Prime Minister attended an evening reception at the Soviet Embassy, an exclusive occasion attended by the élite from politics, art and science. Masses of caviar were consumed and Russian champagne cheered the evening. Even at this date, I was the only photo-journalist present, as an invited guest.

1940 Grave days. Foreign Secretary Anthony Eden talks to Russian Ambassador Maisky at the Foreign Office.

1942 The Lord Mayor's Luncheon. During the war years the traditional Lord Mayor's Banquet became a luncheon. The Prime Minister with the Lord Mayor.

1942 Edouard Beneš. One of several Heads of State who found refuge in Britain, Beneš formed a Czechoslovak Government-in-Exile which he directed from a stately home in England. He often worked at a small table on the lawn, and was well protected by Czech soldiers among the trees surrounding the lawn.

1942 Grand Duchess Adelheid of Luxemburg. The Grand Duchess was another ruler who came to London in the war years, with her family and her Government.

1942 King Haakon of Norway. (Left, above) The King, in exile with his Government in England, presides at a Cabinet Meeting, with his Prime Minister on his right.

1936 Emperor Haile Selassie. (Far left) Deposed by the Italians after the Abyssinian War of 1935–6, the Emperor was in exile in England, living at Bath, until his return to his own country in 1941. He was interested in improvements he could introduce into his own country, and for this purpose visited one Sunday afternoon a modern swimming pool in Roehampton.

1942 King Zog of Albania (Left)

1941 Oliver Lyttelton, later Lord Chandos, Minister for Production.

1941 Ernest Bevin, Minister of Labour 1940–5, Foreign Secretary 1945–51.

1942 Clement Attlee, Deputy Prime Minister under Churchill.

1954 Winston Churchill, in the clothes he customarily wore in the House of Commons.

1951 Lord Beaverbrook, wartime Minister, newspaper tycoon and friend of Churchill.

1941 Herbert Morrison, wartime Home Secretary.

1943 Epstein in his studio. The American-born sculptor Jacob Epstein discarded the academic tradition in the early twenties. Besides large stone and bronze pieces of a religious character, he executed a very large number of portrait busts. Here he is working in his Hyde Park Gate Studio, on a plaster bust of the 'Red Dean', Hewlett Johnson of Canterbury.

1938 Making Anderson shelters, Baldwin Steel Works. With the imminent danger of war, the government ordered the construction of corrugated steel shelters which could be erected in gardens and offered shelter against blast. They were called Anderson shelters, after their inventor.

1942 Harold Turner in the ballet Everyman. During the war years, theatre and ballet continued in London. At that time it was customary to take theatre and ballet photographs at a special session, using additional lighting, and posing particular scenes. Action pictures, taken during a performance or a final rehearsal, were a novelty.

1942 Mona Inglesby in the ballet Everyman.

1942 A scene from the ballet Everyman.

1946 Graham Sutherland and his great 'Crucifixion'. The British painter is examining, through a 'Claude-mirror', the painting which had been commissioned by the Rev. Walter Hussey, Vicar of Northampton.

1946 Henry Moore working on a maquette. Moore, probably the most important sculptor of our time, never followed the academic tradition.

1949 T. S. Eliot. The American-born poet in his office at Faber & Faber, the London publishers.

1949 Martin Heidegger. Heidegger, a pupil of Husserl, the founder of Phenomenology, was Professor at Freiburg University. His great interest was Existentialism; he is seen here outside his cabin, Todtnauberg, Black Forest.

1950 The art expert Bernard Berenson at 'I Tatti', Florence.

1949 Thomas Mann. Mann, master of the German language, and winner of the Nobel prize for literature, wrote novels with a symbolic meaning. Here he is at a reception at his London publishers, Secker & Warburg.

1931 Hôtel des Invalides, Paris, a home for war-invalids.

1931 Afternoon chat with the nurses, Hôtel des Invalides.

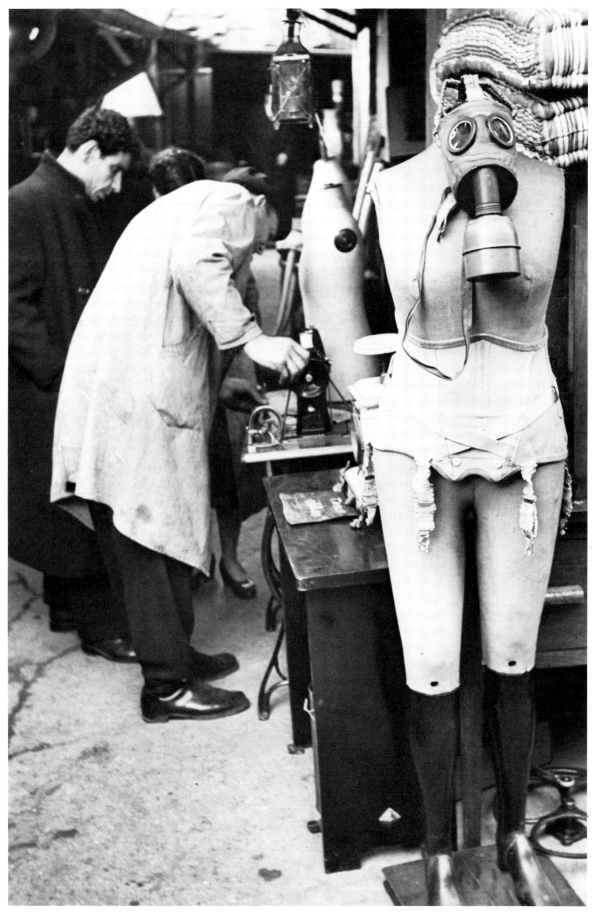

1950 Paris Flea Market. You could find anything and everything at the flea market, and could even discover rarities. The gas-mask and the half-dressed dummy are reminiscent of the German-American painter, Richard Lindner.

1950 Magnificent pieces from the turn of the century, Paris Flea Market.

1950 'Take your choice', Paris Flea Market.

1950 Paris Flea Market. Judging by the size of the dealer, stamps must be good business.

1949 Mining China Clay, Cornwall. China Clay is an important element in the manufacture of art paper for the printing industry. It is mined by being washed down in open-cast.

1949 A handful of China Clay.

1947 **Surrealistic self-portrait.**

Eight European Artists

When I first had the idea of producing my book, in 1948, I did not find it easy to decide who to include. Now, more than 25 years later, the intervening time has shown that the choice was not a bad one. Braque, Chagall, Le Corbusier, Léger, Matisse, Moore, Picasso and Sutherland all still have reputations which have stood the test of time. I would have liked to have included two artists who were approached, but did not wish to cooperate—Rouault and Nolde.

Two British artists were friends of mine, Henry Moore and Graham Sutherland. I had no contact with artists living on the continent. Most artists are well-disposed towards the press, until they become world-famous, when they are apt to reject approaches, making things difficult for photographers. In spite of these problems, I made a start with Matisse in 1948, when he still lived at Vence, a small town in the mountains near Nice.

Henri Matisse

My reception was cool. The painter, now nearly eighty, explained as I started to unpack my camera, that only two or three photographs would be possible, as he could only spare me five minutes. This for me would have been failure. It was impossible for me to take good photographs without first having established some personal contact. Moreover I wanted both colour and black-and-white pictures.

Without responding, I started to repack my equipment back into the cases. When Matisse saw this, impressed by my determination, he at once changed his attitude. He not only gave me the opportunity to take a number of photographs, both black-and-white and colour, but offered to do a new drawing, so that I could photograph the whole process.

When I visited him next, the following year, he had moved to a very large studio-flat in the former Hotel Regina at Nice-Cimiez. Though partly disabled, he worked until almost the end of his life, constantly moving on to new projects. In the last years of his life, when I visited him from time to time, he was much preoccupied with what he regarded as the high point of his work, La Chapelle de Rosaire, St Dominique, in Vence.

When I explained to him the purpose of my projected book, and showed him the results of my previous visits, the painter was most impressed with my colour pictures. 'C'est formidable' he said. 'Vous êtes un artiste—tout cela est très bien—je vais collaborer—c'est une production belle.' His tone was not always as friendly as this. His large studio was of similar dimensions to the chapel at Vence, and the walls were covered with drawings he had made for the chapel; blue, yellow and green panels, with maquettes for stained glass windows were standing to one side. The plan was to transfer these drawings, depicting the life of St Dominique, onto large tiles, to be fired and then used to line the chapel walls, while the sun, filtering through the stained glass, would add colour. One afternoon, while he was sitting in his invalid chair reading a book, I was to experience an outburst of temper. He had heard the click of my camera when he angrily shouted at me 'Vous avez pris ma photographie avec ma bouche ouverte.' I calmed him down, telling him it was some other noise which he had heard; this restored his equilibrium, and I could continue with my work.

He must have been rich in these years, but he did not waste money. The floor of his studio was covered with newspapers to protect it from splashes, something which did not apparently upset his sensibility. Other parts of the flat were furnished with refined taste, with art treasures from New Caledonia and ancient Greece and with precious fabrics on the walls. When he felt well, he would propel himself around the studio in his wheel-chair, working on his designs with a piece of charcoal fixed to the end of a long stick.

About a year later, I called again. It was about eleven in the morning, and he was in bed. He was in poor health, sometimes not getting up for days. But his work spurred him on. He had had a large bed-table made, on which he could go on working. The walls of his room were now lined with *collages* for the colourful vestments for the chapel. These were made of paper, previously coloured by him, cut out and pasted together. While I took some pictures, he dropped asleep. He scarcely slept at night. The darkness and stillness harassed him, and he often left the light and the radio on. I slipped away on this occasion, without disturbing him.

I wanted a hand-written statement from Matisse for my book. He had promised me one, but put it off, always saying 'Next time'. I was in Nice unexpectedly in the summer of 1951, and went to see him. Nobody answered the door, and the concierge told me that the 80-year-old *maître* had gone to Paris, where he still had his old studio on the Boulevard Montparnasse. I was told that Madame Lydia was not with him in Paris, but was on holiday; I called at the Paris studio on my way back to London. A charming girl opened the door. She had seen me in Nice, and recognised me, but apparently had strict instructions to turn all visitors away. 'Matisse n'est pas là' she exclaimed, smiling. 'Il est dans la campagne.' At this moment a door opened at the end of the corridor, and there he was, wearing a tropical suit with a large Panama hat on his head, standing there looking at me like a ghost—Matisse, fresh and lively, as I had not seen him for some time, happy to be in Paris in spite of the heat.

To get the hand-written statement, I had to make another trip to Nice. I took it with me to Menton, where I was to spend the winter. But as soon as I got there, the telephone rang. It was Lydia, asking me to return the manuscript, as Matisse wanted to make some changes. With some presence of mind, I said 'Too late—it is already in the mail to London.' Had I returned it, I might never have seen it again. On the front page, Matisse had written his name in large letters, framed by box-like lines. Was this a premonition that, when the book was published, he would be dead?

The text of his statement read:

'The painter must tackle his subject with no preconceived notions; it is as though he is comtemplating a landscape from which is borne towards him the scent of the earth, the flowers and the fruits of the countryside: he must wait for the breeze to reach him.

The sum of these sensations transmute the subject into a plastic emotion, which the painter is impelled to impress.

I always think that the expressiveness of a work of art depends entirely on the feelings inspired in the artist by the contemplation of his model, and not on exact rendering of the proportions or outward characteristics of the subject.

One must divine in one's model that which goes to make up its interest, disregarding all that does not serve to bring out its essential nature.'

Matisse was an imposing figure. Heavily built, even at 80 he stood firm and erect on his legs. Though no Bohemian, he loved to dress colourfully, and preferred specially-made clothing of a picturesque cut. He usually wore a chestnut-brown suit with very wide sleeves. looking like a wrap. A green waistcoat, sandals and multi-coloured socks completed his daily outfit.

It was often said that Matisse and Picasso were more or less at loggerheads, but this was not true. The two great artists had a life-long friendship. When Matisse died, Picasso said 'No painter understood how to use colour like Matisse—he was the only one who could make a canvas smile and sing.' In the so-called 'atelier d'été', Matisse had paintings and ceramics by Picasso, next to his own works.

Pablo Picasso

When I first visited Picasso he was nearly 70. It was at Vallauris, the pottery town in the south of France, where he lived for several years. His was a modest cottage, slightly above the town, with only a few rooms—his studios were in the town. His life-style was extremely modest, his clothes simple—baggy trousers, a pullover, and a woollen scarf on cool days. His only luxury was an enormous chauffeur-driven American car, nearly as big as his cottage. When he left Vallauris and remarried, this simplicity gave way to a more luxurious style.

His was a very different nature from Matisse. At 70, his vitality was not in the least diminished; he looked at least ten years younger than his age. One could never know in advance what his mood would be. If it was not one of the days when his great intellect and wit bubbled over, he usually did not appear at all, and the visitor had to leave disappointed.

While he was at Vallauris, it was useless to try and make a date in advance. He had no telephone, and would not open letters, on principle. Even if one succeeded in making an appointment, it did not mean much to him. He would change his plans at a moment's notice; he could suddenly decide, in the late afternoon, to mobilise his household and dash off to Paris that evening on the *Train Bleu*. But, if one was lucky and met him on a good day, he could be most kind, and meet all his visitor's wishes sympathetically—even a visitor without a party-membership card.

As a rule, he did not get up until 11. He had built a small fountain in the garden, for his children Claude and Paloma when they were still small children. The terrace around the fountain formed his reception room. If the weather was fine and the sun shining, visitors assembled there, waiting for the *maestro's* appearance. Even in the winter months, Picasso came out sooner or later, wrapped up with a woollen scarf.

Conversation in French ensued for about half-an-hour. The less important visitors were then dismissed, while he walked down to his studios in the town with the favoured few, to display his latest creations: paintings of Claude and Paloma, sleeping or playing; family scenes with Françoise Gilot and the children; sculptures of owls, goats, flowers or female figures. His own ceramics—vases and plates—stood on the shelves, fired at the Madura pottery in the town. Many new drawings and lithographs lay around. One could but wonder how he found time for all this work in so many different fields—and still have time to spend the morning showing his visitor round his studios.

He told me how his friendship had been abused, when two young artists knocked at his door, to show him some work. When they left, one photographed Picasso shaking hands with the other, and published the picture later with the caption 'Picasso congratulates a young painter on his work'.

I visited Picasso at Vallauris seven or eight times. He took me to the pottery; and once we went to the Musée Grimaldi at Antibes. He had lived and worked there for a couple of years, and a lot of his work from this period is preserved as a collection—happy pictures and large drawings of fauns, nymphs and Arcadian scenes, as well as plates and vases.

One morning I walked with Picasso down to the town to take some colour photographs, and he took me into the sculpture-studio. He had built up the scaffolding for a piece of sculpture, the well-known *Goat*, using old bricks, wire and bits of a palm-tree. When I returned to the studio after lunch, to continue my colour records, Picasso recalled me to the sculpture-studio. With an ambiguous smile he exclaimed 'Now, look. I have given the goat sex-symbols.' Between the hind legs of the primitive scaffolding, two small round boot-polish lids were dangling on pieces of wire.

Picasso could be most helpful and cooperative about photography, if his interest was aroused, or if the method was new and he was convinced that it was worth-while. But it was a different matter to get him to put down on paper some of his views on art. Such statements, he said, are only too often misquoted and misused. I tried hard to get Picasso to join the other seven artists who were to be included in my book, and make a written contribution; but he always declined, saying he had never done such a thing before, though he had given his views in conversation from time to time.

When the book was nearly completed, with everything pasted-up in a dummy, including the contributions of the other artists in facsimile, but with the pages reserved for Picasso left blank, I made a final attempt. Picasso was in bed with a cold, at his Paris studio in the Rue des Grands Augustins. I handed the dummy over to his old friend and secretary, Sabartes. He promised to show the book to Picasso, but was very negative about my chances. 'If he does write something, I do not know Picasso, that is all I can tell you' were his last words to me as I left.

I returned to the studio 24 hours later, to collect my dummy. 'It is all there' Sabartes exclaimed, 'Picasso has done it. He had made a design of the whole alphabet on three pages, and he says you may write what you like with the letters.' What this genius had done, simply and true to himself, was to arrange the big letters on the pages so as to form a graphic unity.

Fernand Léger

Fernand Léger, who died in 1955, never found in his lifetime the universal recognition he longed for, something he repeatedly and bitterly deplored. His Montparnasse studio, at the top of an old house without a lift, was large but old-fashioned. There was no electricity or gas; when he wanted to work after dark, he had to light a petrol-lamp, a curious attitude towards technical progress from one who was so progressive in his art. The facilities were the same as when he took over the studio in 1914. He did not want to move, and accepted the discomfort; even the long spiral staircase did not worry him, at the age of 70 or more.

To him, painting was closely related to architecture; he regretted not having studied architecture, and would have preferred this as a profession. 'One of the main innovations in modern architecture' he told me 'has been the creation of a new conception of space. Around 1923 architects had stripped walls of the welter of ornamentation imposed on them by the taste of the 1900s.'

'White walls' he said 'free from ornamentation, now invited experiments with colour. The colouring of wall surfaces modifies one's impression of the appearance and dimensions of the rectangular habitation, a yellow area giving an impression of distance, while red appears closer. The rectangle, hitherto fixed, has become elastic. If this new use of colour is taken to the exteriors of buildings, it could influence the whole character of towns and districts— blue, yellow or green streets enabling us to create new space out of doors, as well as indoors. The matter assumes a wider significance, with social implications: sad grey and black districts, becoming light and gay. Social welfare, so much to the fore at present, can thus find a new outlet, and the problem of town planning, one of the major concerns of 1952, can now be solved.'

Le Corbusier

The great Swiss-born architect, Le Corbusier, would have preferred to have been a painter, as can be seen from the statement he made on 7 August 1951, in his log-cabin at Cap Martin:

'I had to disassociate my paintings from my other creative work, for this painting was contemptuously described by the critics as "bathroom painting" and "quantity surveying". So for 25 years I painted secretly every day from eight in the morning until one o'clock.

Knowing what to paint is the problem; and the answer, how and when and whatever it may be, is found in the mind. A picture I exhibited in 1923 kept me busy every morning for seven months. Yet at Whitsun 1950. I painted two large canvases in three days. The mural in the Pavillon de la Cité, Paris University—a mural of 50 square metres—was completed in nine days, painting at arm's length from the top of a ladder. The themes in that work had been forming in my mind since 1938, in a state of continual ferment until they reached perfection of expression. In the same way, the "Open Hand" theme has clarified in my mind until it has found expression in Chandigarh today, the new capital of the Punjab I am building at the foot of the Himalayas.'

Corbusier was a contradictory person. While he built spacious rooms letting in the fresh air and sunshine through large windows, his private office in the Rue de Sèvres was a dark-painted, windowless, small cubicle. From this gloomy hole he directed his numerous assistants by artificial light. The cubicle, about four metres square, was bare, except for a model of the famous *modulor* hanging on the wall.

Every morning he would run in the Bois de Boulogne for half-an-hour, until his doctor stopped him, as he was over-exerting himself. When at his Cap Martin log-cabin he would jump from the rocks into the sea, until one day he jumped to his death. A great man had passed away.

Marc Chagall

Of all the artists in France, Chagall was the most easy-going. I met him first in the late 1940s, when he lived at Orgeval, near Paris, having returned from America the year before. Like his paintings, which have their own character, quite unlike those of any other artist, poems expressed by luminous colours in an unmistakeable style, Chagall himself was a dreamlike figure of great sensitivity and charm—a painter-poet with all his heart. 'A painting is born into the world like a child, or like the first quickening moment of love. A child is conceived in a second, and a painting is conceived in the mind of the artist in a fraction of time. But before this moment, years must pass; years of gestation, of perfecting, perhaps as each idea grows from theory to reality'.

Seul est mien
Le pays qui se trouve dans mon âme
J'y entre sans passeport
Comme chez moi
Il voit ma tristesse et ma solitude
Il m'endort et me couvre d'une pierre parfumée.'

From Orgeval he soon moved to Vence, the mountain town above the Côte d'Azur, where I became a frequent visitor. This was not only to complete my series of photographs. The city of Frankfurt had tried in vain, through the German Embassy in Paris, to persuade Chagall to paint a large mural for the new Opera House. I became the intermediary, and succeeded in getting Chagall's consent in the end. He not only painted one of his largest works, the *Commedia dell'arte* in glowing colours, but agreed that the fifteen *gouache* sketches should join the painting to hang together in the foyer of the Frankfurt Opera House.

Chagall spoke German, using Yiddish words, and forming sentences as in Yiddish. I visited him for the last time when I wrote a 90th birthday tribute in *Die Welt*. Feeling disturbed by his neighbours, he had left Vence and built a house on a large piece of land at St Paul, where he felt protected from the outside world.

Georges Braque

Braque had two homes, in Paris, near Parc Montsouris Universitaire, and in Normandy, near Varengeville, not far from the beaches where British Commandos landed during the abortive Dieppe Raid of 1942.

His Paris studio was large, very tidy and elegant. The walls were partly covered with large pieces of cloth, golden-brown or rose-coloured. Against these backgrounds, his subdued and rather dark-coloured paintings showed to great advantage. Pieces of native sculpture and masks were about, and large pots with an enormous amount of clean brushes stood on the floor. Unusually, the large studio window faced south and was covered with finely-woven muslin, filtering the sunlight into a warm, soft shadowless light.

Braque had built his cottage at Varengeville in 1931. He went there in summer, staying until the late autumn. There he had two outside studios, in the old garden, facing south. Skylights and windows were covered in the same manner as in the Paris studio. For recreation he used to ride a small motor-cycle into the countryside, where he made sketches in oils. He often mixed his colours himself from powder, kept in numerous pots and tins standing on a large bench in his studio. Everything was neatly arranged, his aesthetic feelings not permitting any disorder. His outdoor sketches were preliminary sketches; but even with these he remained faithful to his principles, which he explained to me as follows:
'I seek to put myself in union with nature, rather than copy her. It is not a matter of reconstructing an anecdote, but of stating a pictorial fact.'

Henry Moore

There seems to be little doubt that Henry Moore has to be considered as one of the most important and influential sculptors of the twentieth century. The significance of Moore's work is emphasised by the fact that his aim is not only the concretion of form; it is far more complex and many-sided than that of Brancusi or Arp, though Arp also aimed at bringing volumes into relationship with space.

In the later war years, he settled in an old farm house at Much Hadham in Hertfordshire. As time has gone on, he has acquired more land, garden, meadows and a small wood. He uses this ground to test the relationship of his sculptures with nature. Sometimes pieces are left in position for six months or more, as he prefers to form his judgements after a long period of study. 'If a piece of sculpture can satisfy in the open air, it can also stand inside, if the room has the proper dimensions—but not *vice versa*, because sculpture standing in the open must be of oversize dimensions.' This is one of the numerous statements made to me by Moore, during my frequent visits over the last 30 years.

Moore's work is not abstract in the sense of being 'non-representational', although in his later years he has gone very far with his abstractions, but even these are always based on nature. *Knife Edged Figure*, for instance, is based on a large piece of bone he dug up in one of his fields, and showed to me.

When walking about his land, and the various studios built on it, Moore likes to explain his work and his principles, and the differences in the various types of sculpture. 'A bronze is a cast made from a model, gradually built up by adding plaster or clay to an armature, while carving in stone or wood is just the opposite. With hammer and chisel one works from the outside towards the inner. What is once cut off is gone for ever.' His is a restless nature, and he likes to move his pieces of sculpture himself, to display them in the best light.

Every afternoon there was family tea, to which guests were invited. After tea one usually moves into a modern sitting room. Moore talks about his work. 'I would say that a sculptor's aim, in fact a sculptor's whole life, is an attempt to understand, to explore the actual form completely in full reality and in three full dimensions. This is a long process—something which cannot be done in a year, nor in two years, nor in ten. It is something that goes on developing all through one's life. It explains why Michelangelo's late work is more real sculpture and shows more understanding of form than his work as a young man, though he was a genius at twenty.'

When, after the war, Moore was working on his stone sculpture *Three Standing Figures*, I followed his progress in a series of photographs. When the sculpture was put up in Battersea Park, I was with him. We had lunch there in the cafeteria, discussing whether painting or sculpture is more important. 'Colour is not important,' he said 'Form is what matters.'

Graham Sutherland

With the other great British artist, Graham Sutherland, the connecting link was friendship dating back to the end of the war. When I included him in my book, his international reputation had not been established. Though a romantic at heart he developed his own style of abstraction, which he followed without deviating, assimilating influences but always remaining Sutherland. His art is based on nature, and is best described in his words to me:

'In painting, the beginning and the end is through the eye. One may go for a walk, and there is everything around one, real yet strange. Certain forms seem to dominate others. I make notes. However brief these may be I can, by this means, take my subject home with me, as it were. In the studio I can remember, from an hour ago, or perhaps from years ago. For me it is always a question of starting with the concrete and recreating something more concrete.'

Sutherland had a fabulous memory for form and colour, and his powers of observation were outstanding. This predestined him as a portrait painter, where his deep feelings and his technical skill were also deployed. His method of painting a portrait was quite different from the usual technique. He started by getting acquainted with his sitter, and tried to establish contact by meeting socially. He was very choosy about his sitters. The majority of his portraits were those of public figures, men with impressive faces and strong characteristics, personalities who had made their mark in their activities or professions. He could afford to make his own choice, as there was a waiting-list of would-be sitters, in spite of the high fees he asked. His reputation as a portrait painter was made with his first portrait—that of Somerset Maugham, painted in the south of France after the war.

I was with him when he painted Beaverbrook. He began with a number of pencil sketches from various angles, to get his bearings. Then he decided on the position in which he was going to paint the sitter. After several more pencil sketches to confirm his choice, he made a life-size oil sketch of the head, followed by a small-scale oil sketch of the whole figure. A photograph taken from precisely the right direction completed his preliminary work, occupying six or eight sittings of an hour each. Several months may then have passed before Sutherland began to work on the actual portrait, usually life size. His amazing memory and ability to visualise the impressions the sitter made on him enabled him to complete the portrait without a further sitting.

Frequently he was attacked for using photographs, although he only used them to check proportions. A painter who cannot paint a portrait without photographs, certainly cannot paint a portrait with photographs; he would produce only a counterfeit, without any inner content. On various occasions, I took photographs for Sutherland; I was with him when he was painting the controversial portrait of Churchill, which the Houses of Parliament presented to the statesman on his 80th birthday.

1949 'La Ruche', Paris. Soutine, Chagall, Léger and Modigliani all lived here, a famous quarter for painters, in their early days.

1950 Pablo Picasso in his studio, Vallauris.

1950 Fernand Léger working on a design in his studio, Montparnasse.

1949 Le Corbusier. The Swiss-French architect in his small cubicle in his working office, Rue de Sèvres, Paris.

949 Marc Chagall. At Orgeval, near Paris, where Chagall first lived after his return from America.

1950 Georges Braque in his Paris studio.

1948 Henri Matisse at home, 'La Rêve', Vence. For my benefit he sat down to draw for me.

51 The ailing Matisse in his day-room in Nice. On the wall were collages for the vestments for the chapel
Vence.

1966 Ossip Zadkine. The Russian-born sculptor came to Paris in 1911; his work, mostly in bronze, shows a certain abstraction.

1950 Académie Léger, Montmartre. The models show great affinity with Léger's work as a painter.

1956 Erich Heckel. Heckel was one of the founders of the 'Die Brücke' group in Dresden in 1905, with Kirchner and Schmidt-Rottluff. The picture was taken in his studio at Hemmenhofen-am-Bodensee.

1967 Barbara Hepworth. Seen here in her sculpture garden, with a friend, at St Ives, Cornwall, Barbara Hepworth was an abstract sculptor who worked in wood, stone and bronze. She had studied in Leeds, where Henry Moore had influenced her, as well as Brancusi. The hollow form plays an important part in her work.

1970 David Hockney with a visitor in his London home. Hockney, the well-known English painter and graphic artist, is a figurative artist who has also painted a number of portraits.

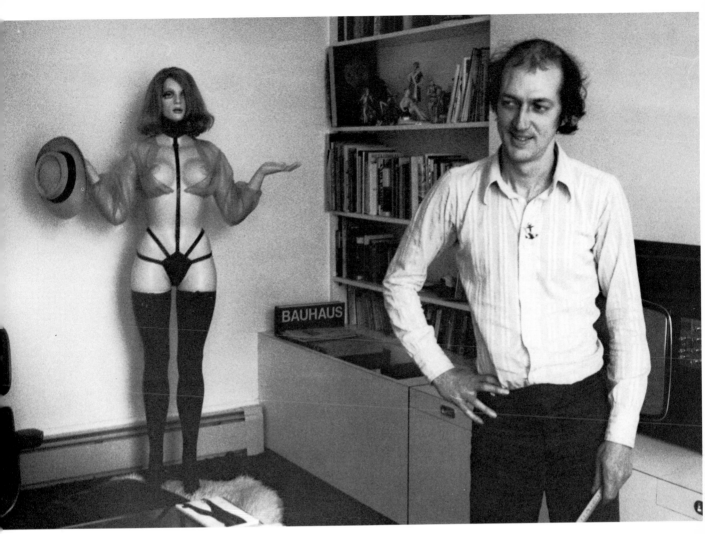

1970 Allen Jones at Home. The English artist's
paintings and sculptures are mostly made from plastic
materials and have an erotic tendency.

1968 André Dunoyer de Segonzac. The French painter and
etcher at his home in St Tropez.

1950 Joan Miró.

1950 Jean-Paul Sartre.

1950 Alberto Giacometti.

1950 Private View at Gallery Maeght, Paris.

1950 Alberto Magnelli.

1950 The German painter Hans Hartung and the French artist Soulages, in Soulages' Paris studio.

1943 Laurence Olivier. The famous actor, now Lord Olivier, in Bernard Shaw's *Arms and the Man*.

1949 George Orwell and his child. In his novel *1984*, Orwell had foretold guided missiles and mind-changing drugs.

1976 Paul Delvaux. The Belgian painter, whose dreamlike surrealistic paintings made him famous, has also executed a number of lithographs.

1967 Marino Marini. The Italian sculptor at his summer home at Forte de Marme with his wife; horse and rider are his principal themes in abstract form.

1969 Giorgio de Chirico. The Italian painter is best known for his Metaphysical paintings.

7 Café Gréco, Rome. Once visited by Goethe, the Café Gréco has retained the style of his day. Chirico, in the centre of this picture, visited the café every day about noon.

1942 The English writer, Evelyn Waugh.

1938 Jacob Epstein at home.

1938 Preparing the boots for Hunting.

1938 Country gentry on the way to the Meet.

1938 Fox-hunting, a favourite country sport, but much criticised.

1938 The Huntsman sounds his horn to signal the end of the day's hunting.

1938 A good glass of beer after an exciting hunt.

1949 A rest on the Grand Canal, Venice.

1950 Amidst the craters of Mount Etna.

1949 Referendum in Trogen. In certain Swiss cantons, a referendum is held when a new law is introduced. Every inhabitant with the right to vote carries a sword.

1950 Woman fetching water, Sicily, still veiled in mid-century.

1930 Children in Sicily. The children are spell-bound by a stranger with a camera, still an attraction at this time.

1950 West Indian English Pomp. A native military band marching through Port-of-Spain.

950 Constitution Day, Port-of-Spain, Trinidad. (Left, above) The Governor-General, Sir Hubert Rance, eads the Queen's proclamation giving the island its own constitution. On the left the Speaker of the Trinidad Iouse of Assembly, in traditional wig.

950 Native Judges listen to the Governor-General's speech. (Left)

1950 Corbeau on pillar, Trinidad. The corbeau, a large bird, acts as a sort of sanitary policeman, eating the remains of all dead animals.

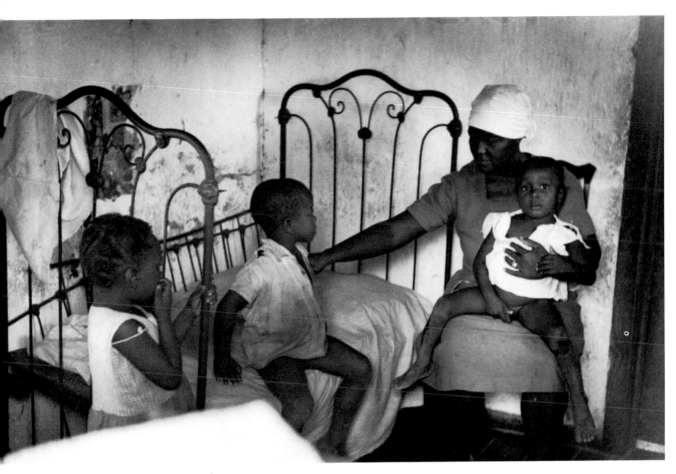

1950 Sugar worker's home, British Guiana. The former British colony is now known as Guyana.

1950 Coconuts are an important industry in the West Indies.

1950 Sugar worker's home, British Guiana.

1950 Sugar worker's kitchen.

1950 Port-of-Spain street scene, Trinidad.

Lunch with Sir Winston Churchill

Churchill was a difficult sitter. The expression on his face changed from minute to minute, as his mood changed. Sometimes he posed, showing what he considered to be an impressive face, as we know it from some of his posed photographs. His eyes moved about continuously, scrutinising.

While Sutherland was at work, Churchill the painter was eager to find out how 'the other painter' was working, what methods he used, and how he handled paint. He had knowledge and experience of painting, and wished to investigate the artistic perceptions of a younger generation, having studied with the representatives of an earlier age, W. R. Sickert and Sir William Nicholson, both post-impressionists.

Churchill's country home, Chartwell, near Westerham in Kent, is less than 35 miles from London. The sittings took place there, in a cottage in the grounds which served the Prime Minister as a studio.

I was supposed to take some photographs of Churchill towards the end of the late-morning sitting, which was supposed to last 50 minutes. Sutherland and I arrived about 12.30 and were greeted by Detective-Sergeant Murray, Churchill's 'shadow', who led us down the few hundred yards to the studio. The 'old man' had not yet appeared, so I was able to examine the studio thoroughly. Both rooms were lined with oil sketches from floor to ceiling, all of them works by the Premier himself, landscapes and still-lifes, most of them in a low colour-key, typical of English post-impressionist painting.

Having looked at the sketches and drawings Sutherland had made at earlier sittings with Churchill, we fixed the position from which I was to photograph, with the detective acting as stand-in, sitting in Churchill's chair.

The sound of a car heralded the arrival of the octogenarian, who took great care of himself and therefore used a car for the short journey from the house to the studio. He was dressed in the sombre garb he wore in the House of Commons—black jacket, striped trousers, and a blue-spotted bow-tie, the clothes he was to wear in the portrait. He would have preferred to wear his robes as a Knight of the Garter, but the House wished him to be portrayed as he had been, for a life-time, in the House of Commons.

After a brief introduction, I started at once with my photographs; as everything was well prepared, it did not take long. We had both been invited to lunch; while Sutherland worked on his sketches, I used the intervening time to look around the garden, swimming pool and pergola, including much of Sir Winston's work as a bricklayer.

As Lady Churchill was away, lunch was an intimate occasion, *à trois*. In the usual English way, we first had a drink in the drawing room, sherry or whisky. Then, while Churchill went upstairs in the special small lift which had been installed for him, we mounted the stairs, passing Sir William Orpen's large portrait of Churchill on the way. Lunch was taken in a small dining room on the first floor, with Churchill at the head of the table, flanked by Sutherland and myself.

It was 31 August 1954; not a very good day, as it was clear that the Prime Minister was rather cross. Though naturally affairs of state were not discussed, it was well known that the French Chamber of Deputies had, against his wishes, rejected a proposal to allow Germany to rearm. He also complained of a sore throat, and insisted that his doctor, Lord Moran, should come to Chartwell that afternoon to paint his throat. But, avoiding politics, there was plenty to talk about, and a stimulating discussion about painting ensued, helped along by a couple of bottles of fine Hock, followed by an old port and equally mature brandy.

'Painting' Churchill said 'is a wonderful method of relaxation. One forgets one's troubles. Everybody ought to try it. My Sergeant is also a painter—when we were in Morocco, we often painted back-to-back. Composing a picture is like planning a battle—both need to be thought over and well prepared.'

What a gifted man he was—politician, writer, orator with a convincing power, a better-than-amateur painter—an all-inspiring personality. A number of his paintings were hanging in the dining room. I was particularly struck by a still-life with bottles and glasses, and told Churchill so; possibly he was impressed by this tribute, because he chose this picture to send to the next Summer Exhibition of the Royal Academy, of which he was an Honorary Member.

A Prime Minister's luncheon does not pass without interruption. A secretary repeatedly came into the dining room with questions; he was called to the telephone several times; Lord Moran's visit was arranged and a throat specialist consulted on the telephone; a Cabinet Meeting was arranged for the next day. During the meal, Churchill looked at my book, *Eight European Artists*, which I had given to him as a pre-birthday present. His poodle, Rufus, was as surly as his master, possibly because I was sitting in the chair he usually occupied.

My proposal to photograph him presiding at a Cabinet Meeting at 10 Downing Street was flatly refused, though I pointed out that this would be of the greatest interest to posterity. 'Impossible' Churchill said. 'It has never been done'. 'It is for precisely that reason that it should be done now' I replied. Though the word 'impossible' did not usually exist in Churchill's mind, in this case he insisted on it, most regrettably.

I had hoped to have a chance of taking a few photographs in privacy. But the day was a bad one; neither Sutherland's charm nor my own efforts could put the Premier at ease. My chance came after lunch, when Churchill had lit one of the outsize Coronas especially made for him in Havana, and had settled down in an arm-chair, resting comfortably and half asleep. There was a large mirror on the opposite wall. When I saw all three of us in this mirror, I was instantly able to record this scene with my small camera. A few moments later, Churchill retired for his usual afternoon rest.

About ten days later, we paid another visit to Chartwell. This time, it was at a more favourable time, in the afternoon, as Churchill usually became livelier as the day progressed; Lady Churchill was present, which had a calming influence. The Prime Minister was wearing a brand-new 'siren-suit', a garment he had started using in the war years. Coat and trousers were made in one piece. with a zip-fastener running down the whole front; this model was made of worsted, with a pale blue pin-stripe. Knowing he was to be photographed, he held one of his Havanas in his hand. He was in great form; one was astounded to learn that he had passed through a serious crisis in his health a few months earlier. While Sutherland studied Churchill's expression, I managed to take some very interesting colour photographs.

When, a few weeks later, I asked permission for one of these pictures to appear on the birthday-anniversary number of *Picture Post*, I received the following reply from Downing Street:

Dear Mr Man,

The Prime Minister has asked me to thank you for your letter of October 4 and for sending him a colour print of one of the photographs you took when you visited Chartwell with Mr Graham Sutherland.

The Prime Minister regrets that he cannot give permission to use these photographs for Press purposes or for any other than that for which they were taken. As you will understand, the Prime Minister receives many requests from photographers to take such pictures and he has been unable to give sittings.

Yours sincerely,

O. P. B. Pitblado

Sutherland too did not have a success with the final portrait. Churchill disliked it, and tried to prevent the official presentation on his birthday. The painting was, however, handed over, only to disappear into the cellar of his house in Hyde Park Gate, and later to be destroyed. Sutherland once said 'Two expressions dominate Churchill's face: one of a bulldog and the other of a cherub.'

Some years later, at the end of the Fifties, I saw Churchill again in the *Salle Privée* of the Monte Carlo Casino. He was sitting at the green table in his wheel-chair, with his host Onassis beside him. From a middle-sized pile of chips, he placed his stake on various numbers, waiting eagerly, with a child-like expression, to see where the little white ball would fall. A big smile spread over his face when he won; when he had lost, and his pile of chips had shrunk, Onassis conjured from his pocket a fresh supply to put in front of Churchill.

1954 Winston Churchill in his own studio, Chartwell.

1954 A photograph through a mirror. After lunch the Prime Minister, rather tired, settled down in an arm chair with his large cigar. The picture, taken through the mirror opposite, shows Churchill, the painter Graham Sutherland and Felix H. Man.

Konrad Adenauer

Always interested in international exchange of culture, I suggested, in the winter of 1958, to Hans von Herwarth, the German Ambassador in London, that Graham Sutherland should paint a portrait of the German Chancellor, Konrad Adenauer. Von Herwarth, very much in favour of the proposition himself, made the necessary contact with Bonn, only to get the answer that seven requests of this kind had already been made by various artists and Sutherland therefore would be eighth in line. However, neither von Herwarth nor myself gave in and rather tenacious negotiations with Secretary of State Globke in Bonn followed and von Herwarth arranged a meeting between the Chancellor and Sutherland during one of his visits to London.

Sutherland had recently painted a portrait of Prince Egon of Fürstenberg, in Donaueschingen. A reproduction of this in colour impressed Adenauer and, in the end, he agreed to sit for Sutherland during his holiday in Cadenabbia in May 1959. The German Press got onto this story and pestered Sutherland and myself with telephone calls—hoping for a scoop. Neither of us gave any information about this secret project. At this time Sutherland was engaged on the huge tapestry he had designed for Coventry Cathedral and the German Press, in order to have news of some kind, printed a statement that Sutherland was engaged for six weeks with *Tapetenentwürfen*, translating tapestry as 'wall-paper'. This alleged statement by Sutherland was regarded as an affront in Bonn, and everthing was called off. Further requests had no more success; but I did not give up, and was finally told by Secretary of State Globke, in March 1963, that Chancellor Adenauer would be ready for the first sitting on April 6, at Cadenabbia, on Lake Como.

Everything was arranged accordingly, with rooms booked in Lugano, when Mrs Sutherland telephoned on April 5 to say that the artist was in bed with a severe attack of 'flu; years of effort had been destroyed by a few microbes. However, after further correspondence with Bonn, a new date was made for September, also in Cadenabbia. For some years Adenauer had come to Cadenabbia when in need of rest. He always stayed at the Villa Collina, a large private house in a large park. Guards patrolled the iron fence around the estate, and the entrance was controlled by police from the Trentino district, bilingual in German and Italian.

When Sutherland and I called at the villa, we could sense a farewell mood, as this was to be Adenauer's last holiday there before his retirement as Chancellor. The weather was cool, and the sittings took place on a covered terrace, with splendid views of Lake Como and the Engadine Alps. As usual, Sutherland sketched in pencil and in oils. Adenauer was an excellent and easy-going model, who could keep a position without effort. A lively conversation went on, with Adenauer explaining his political views to the Englishman; he was rather exasperated with Britain and disappointed with Macmillan, but strongly for De Gaulle. He spoke no English, so either myself or his secretary interpreted.

'Before I return to Germany' he said 'I am going to Rome to see Pope Paul VI. I want to hear at first hand what position the Pope intends to take about the threat of Communism. His predecessor, Pope John, was far too easy-going about this danger threatening Europe.' He also intended visiting De Gaulle at Rambouillet to discuss international relationships, and especially the Test-Ban Treaty. 'Germany cannot get on without the support of the U.S.A.' he declared. 'But we must weigh Kennedy's approach to Khruschev very carefully on the scales.'

During the eight days on which sittings took place, the conversation moved from politics to art. Adenauer understood how to adjust his views to current trends, but he had no feeling whatever for the art of his own time. Not even the Impressionists meant much to him; but he loved the work of Old Masters and was glad to talk about his collection of paintings—primitives of the Cologne School, Titian, El Greco and Velasquez.

When I told Adenauer I had published a book entitled *Eight European Artists*, he wanted to know the names of the artists I had included. When I told him, he said 'You must be convinced that they are all great artists.' 'Naturally so' I replied. 'I cannot take Picasso seriously' Adenauer said. 'He makes fun of the world. I do not understand his art, nor that of Chagall. For me, great art came to an end with Delacroix.'

As a practising Catholic, Adenauer attended Mass in the village church on Sunday. We did the same. Though terrorism as it flourishes today hardly existed at this time, detectives made a thorough examination of the church, even searching the confessional. When the big black Mercedes made its appearance, the people gave way respectfully. Adenauer was held in high esteem in Cadenabbia. There was a firework display in his honour at the lakeside. We were invited by Adenauer to join him in the motor-launch provided for the occasion by the local council. We cruised in the magic evening light, and drank the great man's health in champagne.

Eighteen months later, without any further sittings, Sutherland completed the portrait. The main portrait was a life-sized whole figure; there was also a head-and-shoulders and some sketches. The paintings were taken to Bonn and showed to Adenauer in the room he used in the Bundeshaus after his resignation as Chancellor. Sutherland was not present. The large portrait had been placed on a stand; Adenauer sat silently looking at the picture for a while. 'Yes' he said 'I like it. Mr Sutherland has painted me as a thinking human being.' He got up to look at the smaller portrait, and turned to the Secretary of State von Herwarth, the former Ambassador. 'Can we keep the paintings for a few days? I want to show them to my family, to my children, and I want my 23 grandchildren to see their grandfather as a thinker.'

Adenauer, pleased with the portraits, showed me his personal treasures—a small oil by Churchill, a genuine Eisenhower next to it, a large photograph of De Gaulle in a silver frame, with a dedication, and a beautiful Gothic madonna in a corner of the room. When I left, he invited me to visit him at his home at Rhöndorf when I was next in Bonn, an invitation he repeated later in writing.

In the autumn of 1978 an exhibition of the Adenauer portraits and sketches Sutherland had painted was arranged at the house of the Adenauer foundation at St Augustin near Bonn. At the same time all the various photographs I had taken in Cadenabbia and Trottiscliffe were on view. Sutherland and myself were present. After the inauguration we joined the President of the Federal Republic Scheel and his successor Carstens together with other dignitaries at a luncheon party.

1963 Konrad Adenauer, Chancellor of the Federal Republic of Germany, at his holiday retreat, Cadenabbia, Lake Como.

1963 Graham Sutherland sketching Adenauer at Cadenabbia.

1964 Graham Sutherland's studio at Trottiscliffe, Kent, with various versions of the Adenauer portrait.

Discussion at 10 Downing Street. The Prime Minister, Harold Macmillan, talking to Lord Hailsham.

1949 King Bhumibol of Thailand, with his bride Princess Sirikit, on the occasion of their engagement, Lausanne.

50 Pope Pius XII. After celebrating Mass in St Peter's during Holy Year, the Pope leaves in ancient style and all ꞅomp accompanied by his guard of honour.

1963 Pope John XXIII at a Lenten street procession. In those days, it was possible for a Pope to join such a procession without any risk.

1974 Pope Paul VI in the Church of Saint Sabina, Rome, on Ash Wednesday.

1978 Pope John Paul II at his enthronement. A photograph taken from television—the photo-journalist as armchair photographer.

New Activities

After my experimental year with the *Sunday Times* in the late Fifties, I grew less interested in photography. I used my camera only when I met an important personality, artist, writer or politician, or when personally interested in a scene. My view was that photo-journalism as such had reached a dead-end. Naturally some splendid individual pictures were still being taken for publication. But the old vigour and spirit, current in the early days when the photo-journalist was his own master, using a camera instead of a pen, was gone. Now the written word dominated the photography. In *Life* magazine's editorial offices, synopses were drawn up, giving the photographer directions for the story, and the editor was delighted when he received hundreds of pictures from which he could choose.

My main interests were in the visual arts. As lithography became of increasing interest to collectors, it was no longer possible, as in my early days, to pick up masterpieces of the art for a trifling sum. My second book on this art was published in 1970, by Studio-Vista in London and by Putnam in New York; this was a world history of lithography from Senefelder to the present day, *Artists' Lithographs*. The Print Council of America commissioned me to assemble a *catalogue raisonné* of the first ten years of lithography in England (1801–1810), where the art was first developed. Several years went into *The Complete Graphic Work of Graham Sutherland, 1922–1969*, which was published in three languages by the Galerie Wolfgang Ketterer of Munich.

When I reached the age when other people retire and feeling, even after 25 years, that the English climate did not really suit me very well, I decided to return to the continent. I moved to Lugano; from here I could conduct my new activity as editor of a new publication I had founded with Galerie Wolfgang Ketterer. *Europaeische Graphik* consisted of large portfolios of ten original graphics in limited editions. At that time the flood of modern graphics had not swamped the market. We insisted that each artist had to do the work involved themselves, without the assistance of professional lithographers or etchers, so that what we published were genuinely 'original graphics'. This is a principle not in vogue today. As editor, it was my task to select the artists, visit them for a preliminary talk, and later on to supervise the printing, signing and numbering. A lot of travelling was involved, and Lugano proved to be a good starting-point. Altogether we published ten portfolios, and the venture brought me into contact with artists all over Europe.

As the years went by, my own collection of artists' lithographs became a comprehensive one, from the very earliest days to the present. Several museums became interested in the collection; in 1971 it was shown in Germany and Switzerland, and for three months at the Victoria and Albert Museum in London, for which I assembled a lavishly-illustrated reference catalogue. The collection is now in the new Graphics Department in the National Gallery in Canberra.

Frequent visits from Lugano across the border into Italy, often to Rome, prompted me to move further south to the Holy City, where I had found a small penthouse in the old city. Over the years I had contributed often on cultural affairs to the *Düsseldorfer Handelsblatt*. I now became a regular contributor to *Die Welt*, the large German daily paper, sometimes illustrating my articles with my own photographs. For many years I have also been kept busy arranging exhibitions of my photographs all over Europe and America, compiling catalogues which have appeared in seven languages.

During my years in London, I had done some thorough research into the origins of the illustrated newspaper; the partly-finished typescript is waiting in a drawer to be taken out some day . . .